Make an eBook

The complete handbook for creating, marketing and selling eBooks successfully

Michael Boxwell

Greenstream Publishing

Greenstream Publishing

Greenstream Publishing
12 Poplar Grove
Ryton on Dunsmore
Warwickshire
CV8 3QE
United Kingdom

www.greenstreampublishing.com

Published by Greenstream Publishing 2011

ISBN 978-1-907670-11-4

Editor: Angela Boxwell
Cover Photograph: Spencer Parry

Michael Boxwell asserts the moral right to be identified as the author of this work.

A catalogue record for this book is available from the British Library.

While we have tried to ensure the accuracy of the contents in this book, the author or publishers cannot be held responsible for any errors or omissions found therein.

Table of Contents

Chapter 1: Introduction

This is a guide to creating and selling eBooks. I have written it for authors and for people who are serious about writing.

If you have a writing talent, plus a passion and an ability to communicate through your writing, this guide will help you make your work is as successful as possible.

Producing eBooks is not complicated or difficult, but there are some traps for the unwary. For the book itself, you need to focus on quality. To promote your book successfully, you need to create a plan and follow it through to completion.

Of course, I cannot promise to make your eBook into a best seller. Yet the techniques I describe in this guide and the steps I propose have worked many times before, creating best sellers even with unknown or previously unpublished authors.

What this guide covers

This guide looks at the eBook market, reveals who is buying them and explains why eBooks are becoming so successful. It describes the different formats for eBook production. It gives reasons as to why you may want to create an eBook yourself and then explains the technicalities of producing one and getting it on sale.

As some authors have found, however, getting an eBook on sale is not the problem. Many authors have found that they go through all the steps for producing an eBook, only to find that they do not even sell one copy. Therefore, this guide suggests some straightforward, low-cost steps to promote your eBook. These steps will get your eBook noticed by your potential customers and improve your sales.

What this guide does not cover

The guide also does not tell you what you should write about or how to get started in the writing profession. It also does not tell you how to write, proofread or edit a book.

The guide starts from the point where you have already completed your manuscript and want to launch it as an eBook.

I am assuming that you know how to do most common tasks on your word processor, such as creating a table of contents, configuring paragraph layouts and running your spell checker.

Think Quality

Unfortunately, many websites claim that you can 'easily' write an eBook, publish it in just a couple of days and make a fortune from it. Unfortunately, this is just not true.

Whilst it is possible to write an eBook and earn a rewarding additional income from it, it does require a talent for writing. You book must also be properly proof-read. You will also require commitment, patience and time in order to make it a commercial success.

I have read articles that claim you can cut out professional proof-reading and editing by asking your friends to do it for you. In reality, you are going to end up with a sub-standard book if you choose to do this.

Book retailers may refuse to sell your book if it is sub-standard. If you do happen to get a sub-standard book on sale, you will certainly receive critical reviews and this will stop your book becoming successful. Focus on quality; make sure you get the book right. It will be worth it in the end.

A few terms

When I refer to an *e-reader*, I am talking about a physical device such as a Kindle, laptop computer or mobile phone.

When I refer to a *Reader*, I am talking about a human being reading your book.

About me

My name is Michael Boxwell. I am a professional author with ten published books and several eBooks to my name.

I wrote and released my first eBook in 1991. It was a humorous book written for computer programmers and distributed amongst friends. To my utter amazement, the book gained several thousand readers. Back then, eBooks were text files and readers printed them out onto computer printout paper to read them. They were most often distributed via floppy disk or using electronic 'bulletin boards'.

My background covers technology and business. I have run a number of successful small businesses and have learnt the value of simple, low-cost and effective marketing. I have adapted many of these skills to promoting my own books. I also regularly advise other authors on the best ways to promote their books.

Today, most of my writing is about environmental technology. Amongst other things, I have written books on solar power and electric car use. Within their niches, several of these books have become worldwide best sellers, both in printed and eBook form.

Chapter 2: The history of eBooks

Most people assume that eBooks are a relatively new invention. In fact, the origins of eBooks can be traced back to 1970 with a prototype computer called the *Dynabook*. This was a proposed general-purpose handheld computer with an electronic book reading system.

American author and computer enthusiast, Michael S. Hart, wrote and released the first eBook back in 1971. Hart saw that computers had the potential to change the way people read books, with fast indexing facilities and the ability to add more books without increasing the physical space required to keep them.

Early eBooks tended to be technical books and computer manuals. By the end of the 1970s, many software packages incorporated eBooks as electronic help systems. Car manufacturers were also using computers for providing technical information on their cars.

eBooks continued to have a small but dedicated band of followers until the mid 1990s. By then, Michael Hart had converted around 1,000 books to electronic format, including the bible and many of the eminent literary classics. The availability of these books on the Internet did much to engage the public's interest. Authors who had works that had not been accepted by publishers started to distribute their works as eBooks.

Meanwhile, products like Microsoft Encarta, a reference book distributed on CD, showed people how useful computers were for research purposes, allowing people to find what they wanted at the touch of a button.

By now, the lack of suitable hardware was holding back the uptake of eBooks. People did not want to sit at a desk reading a novel on their PC screen. Nor did they want a bulky laptop. What the public wanted was an electronic e-reader similar in size and weight to a paperback book.

The first true e-readers appeared in 1998. Three companies: Rocket, SoftBook and Cytale all launched handheld e-readers whose primary purpose was to read books. Customers could download books from their PC, or in the case of the SoftBook, by connecting the unit to a phone jack and connecting into the Internet.

These early units were expensive, heavy, and had a battery life of only two or three hours. Yet they demonstrated there was a market for the technology and improvements were made. By the middle of the decade, smaller and lighter e-readers with battery life measured in hundreds of hours were available.

In the latter half of the last decade, Sony and Amazon took the market lead for e-readers. With lighter, cheaper and better e-readers finally available, customers started buying in larger numbers.

Today, e-readers have come of age and the eBook has become a popular way to read. They offer consumers the convenience of an entire library of books at the touch of a button, long battery life, clear screens, the ability to scale text to any size and let readers get hold of new books within seconds.

It is no surprise then that eBook sales are rocketing. Many experts are predicting that they will replace printed books within the next decade.

Chapter 3: eBooks today

Between 1980 and 2000, book sales were in a slow but steady decline. Consumers were spending their leisure time doing other activities. People eschewed books for other pastimes such as watching films and playing computer games.

Then the publishing industry began to fight back. A new style of writing began to emerge. Publishers looked for new genres. Shorter novellas became popular (a novella is a short novel) and the now infamous *chick-lit* arrived. Fresh and compelling marketing encouraged young people to try these new books. Consumers of all ages responded and sales began to grow once more.

Today, book sales in general are on the rise. From the late 1990s until 2010, paperback book sales constantly grew by around 5% each year. That has been impressive growth for a subdued worldwide economy.

Yet that growth is nothing compared to eBook sales. From small sales two years ago, the growth in eBook sales has been nothing short of monumental.

In July 2010, Amazon was claiming that eBooks were outselling hardback books and accounted for around 8½% of all books sold. Just six months later, in January 2011, Amazon announced that eBooks now accounted for 45% of all book sales and that eBooks outsold paperback books. For every 100 paperback books that Amazon sold in January 2011, they sold 115 eBooks.

Since then, the eBook market has grown even more. By the end of April, 2011, Amazon said eBooks now outsold both paperback and hardback books combined. Based on Amazon's sales, eBooks had a 52½% market share and were continuing to grow month-on-month.

If these figures are replicated across the rest of the industry, this would suggest that over $1.1 billion of eBooks are sold worldwide each month. This compares to sales of $19 million per month at the end of 2009.

eBook Sales growth between 2004 and 2010

eBook sales growth has been nothing short of astronomical. Ignore the figures, a simple chart shows the scale of growth over the past few years:

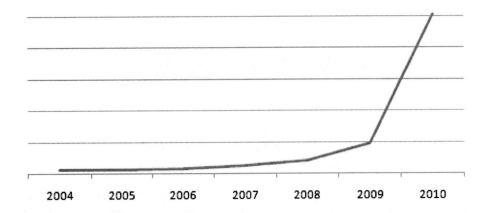

The size of this market simply cannot be ignored. If you are an author and your books are not available in eBook format, you are missing out on a substantial market.

How to read an eBook

There is a wide variety of devices available on which to read eBooks. They can be read on desktop or notebook computers, on dedicated e-readers, on iPads, iPhones or iPods and on many mobile phones.

The most popular dedicated e-reader available today is the Amazon Kindle. This is a compact, lightweight unit with a battery life of several hundred hours. It weighs less than a paperback book and has a crisp, clear screen that can be comfortably read wherever you are. It can connect directly to the Amazon online bookshop via wi-fi or mobile phone link and can keep an estimated 3,500 books in its memory.

How people read eBooks

Some people read eBooks as a replacement to printed books. Others read them alongside printed books. Some people download eBooks onto a mobile phone, so they always have a book with them when they are on the move.

eBook formats

There are several different formats for reading eBooks. They all have different characteristics each with their own benefits and drawbacks:

PDF

PDF is the industry standard for technical books and for information meant to be read on a PC screen. It is also the best format for documents that are to be printed out. PDF takes a standard page layout and produces it exactly as an electronic version.

Whilst this is acceptable with a PC, it does not work with a smaller screen. In too many cases, PDF documents are simply unreadable on an e-reader or a mobile phone display. For this reason, they are losing popularity to other, more flexible formats.

EPUB

EPUB is supposed to be the emerging standard for eBook publication. All e-readers support EPUB and many booksellers sell EPUB format eBooks. Unfortunately, there are problems with EPUB books as different e-readers interpret the format slightly differently. This can cause problems when formatting an EPUB eBook.

Consequently, it is difficult to predict how your book will look when used on different e-readers. This is especially true of diagrams, images and tables, which may render well on one unit but be entirely unreadable on another.

Amazon is the biggest bookseller in the world, and the biggest retailer of eBooks. The biggest issue for the EPUB format is that Amazon does not supply EPUB format books. Instead, they offer all their books in their own format.

Kindle (previously called MOBI)

Amazon comfortably leads the world in eBook sales. As well as selling the Kindle e-reader, they have created free Kindle reading software for many other devices. These include mobile phones, the Apple iPad, iPhone and iPod, Windows based PCs and the Apple Mac.

Compared to EPUB books, Kindle books are much easier to create. You can be much more confident that they will work well on any device using the Kindle reading software.

The only dedicated e-reader that you can use to read Kindle eBooks is the Amazon Kindle. If you have a Sony e-reader or a B&N Nook, you cannot read eBooks formatted in the Kindle format.

Nevertheless, Kindle eBooks are now the strongest selling eBook format around the world, and look likely to remain so for some time to come.

Chapter 4: Why should I make an eBook?

If you are an author with a number of titles already on sale, you need to ensure they are available in eBook format. If they are not, you are quite simply losing sales.

I know people who will ignore a book if it is not available as an eBook. Instead of buying your printed book, they will choose an eBook written by someone else instead. So let me repeat: if your current books are not available as eBooks, you are losing sales.

Some authors and publishers use eBooks in other ways. Older books that are no longer in print can be re-released in eBook form. The sales volume may not warrant a print run and distribution, but may still provide enough revenue to be worthwhile as an eBook alone.

Alternatively, some authors re-release older books as free or low-cost eBooks to encourage new readers to try their works. If the reader enjoys reading a free book from the back catalogue, he or she is more likely to buy a paid-for book from the same author.

Some well-known authors write short stories as eBooks that they give away or sell for a small amount of money. These short stories can persuade the public to try out a book from an author they otherwise would not have chosen.

If you want to expand your market for your books, you can use an eBook as a springboard to create a global audience for your work. Unlike printed books, eBooks are not just limited to one or two countries. eBooks sell across the world. If you are an author and want to create a worldwide following, eBooks can be an excellent way of achieving this.

If you are not yet a published author, an eBook gives you the opportunity to be 'discovered' by the public. It allows you to gain a following. A successful eBook can help you create a reader base for your future works and can help you build your credibility with publishers.

However, if you are not yet a published author, make sure that what you are releasing is genuinely good enough to put on sale. Writing a book can be hard work, but publishing it and promoting it successfully will also require a lot of effort. If what you have written is sub-standard, you will soon get poor or mediocre reviews and damage your reputation.

Get your book professionally proof-read and edited. If the occasional error creeps in to your text, that is understandable. If every page has mistakes, you will soon end up with unhappy readers.

If you cannot afford to get your book professionally proof-read or edited, use an online proof-reading tool such as grammarly.com. Whilst it is not a substitute for a good editor, it does do an excellent job of highlighting problems that are otherwise all too easy to miss. You can register for a seven day free trial at www.grammarly.com.

Will eBook sales reduce sales of existing paperback or hardback titles?

No. Right now, eBook sales are currently incremental to printed book sales.

People who own an e-reader want the book of their choice in eBook format. If your book is not available, those people will buy someone else's rather than buy a printed book. Right now, when you make your book available as an eBook, you still sell just as many paperback and hardback books.

Of course, at some point, eBook sales will reduce sales of paperback or hardback titles: the astronomical growth of the market will ensure that is the case sooner rather than later.

How do I stop people making rip-off copies of my book?

Today, it is as easy to get rip-off copies of films as it is to get the real thing. The same is true of music. So how do you stop rip-off copies of your eBook appearing around the Internet?

This is an issue within the industry, with many publishers and authors concerned that there will be widespread illegal copying of their work. It is true that they may well lose some sales as a result, but research into this suggests that most of the music, films and books that are illegally downloaded are never used. This suggests that people do not appreciate what they copy illegally. In most cases, these people would not have paid for that product in the first place.

Of course, in relation to printed books, it has been possible to read books without paying for them for a long time. Libraries exist for this very purpose. People lend books to their friends or swap them when they have finished with them. As authors, we do not object to that.

Quite possibly, some books sell fewer copies because of lending libraries. Just as possibly, some books sell in higher numbers as readers discover new authors. My point is this: it is unlikely that a few illegal copies will make much difference to the success of your book.

Some authors have gone a step further: they have provided a free copy of their book on their website, so that it can be read by anyone with an Internet connection free of charge. Some of these books have gone on to become best sellers, despite also being available at no cost.

There is protection available for eBooks, in the form of *Digital Rights Management* (DRM). You can choose to build DRM into your eBook as part of the publishing process. When a customer buys an eBook with DRM, they have to register the book with their PC and e-reader in order to read it.

Digital Rights Management allows a buyer to put the eBook on up to five devices at a time. However, if they try to distribute it to friends or family, or post it up on the Internet, then the eBook is useless to the recipients.

Digital Rights Management does extend to eBook lending libraries. An eBook in a library can be downloaded by a reader for a certain period. When that time has expired, the eBook can no longer be read by that person. Whilst the eBook is out on loan, it is not available for other people to read.

Digital Rights Management is unpopular with many people, who think it is a restriction on their liberties. These people argue that they can lend paperback books to friends, so why can they not lend eBooks to friends in the same way? There have also been technical issues: in order to read DRM books, you need to have the right software on your PC and some of this software has been difficult, cumbersome or even downright impossible to use.

In reality, it is this second reason that is causing the problems. EPUB format books with DRM sell in much smaller volumes because the software to open a DRM book is so difficult to use.

Amazon has resolved both of these problems, with an invisible Digital Rights Management system and the Kindle lending facility. If you have an eBook that you want to lend to someone else, you can lend it for a few weeks, direct from your Kindle or your PC. Once the time is up, the eBook is automatically returned to you and you can read it again.

Whilst I hear people complain about DRM on EPUB books all of the time, I have never heard anyone ever complain about DRM on Kindle books. It is just not seen as an issue.

It is up to you whether you want to incorporate Digital Rights Management for your books or not. Authors who have not included Digital Rights Management have not reported widespread illegal distribution of their titles, but there is always the possibility that this could change in the future.

How much money could I hope to make selling eBooks?

That depends entirely on how much you sell your eBook for and how many you sell. Customers perceive that eBooks are free to distribute, so should be cheaper to buy than printed books. Book retailers have been keen to push the price of eBooks down in order to increase their own sales, but traditionally have also offered modest revenues for authors and publishers.

That is all changing with Amazon's new strategy of providing a significantly bigger chunk of revenue to authors selling low-cost books. If you sell a title for under $9.99 in the United States (£6.99 in the United Kingdom), then Amazon will give you a 70% share of the profit margin on the book. If you sell a title for more than $9.99, then Amazon will give you only a 35% share of the pre-tax retail price on the book.

Note the difference between profit and retail price. If you go for the 70% share, then Amazon will charge you a small amount – typically $0.01-$0.10 – per book sold for the delivery fee: i.e. for the cost of the eBook transfer through the Amazon website. Amazon also reserves the right to discount your eBook and pay you less, based on the lower sales price of the eBook.

If you go for the 35% royalty, you get a 35% royalty on the pre-tax retail price of the book. If Amazon chooses to discount the book to promote it, then you still receive your 35% royalty based on the list price. 35% royalty books also do not pay the Amazon delivery charge.

Incidentally, these prices exclude sales tax. In the UK, printed books are exempt from Value Added Tax (VAT). However, eBooks are not exempt from VAT. Therefore, if you set the price at £6.99 for the UK, the list price that customers pay is £8.39.

For non-fiction books, eBooks should be between 20-35% cheaper than their paperback equivalents.

For fiction books, people also expect to pay less for the eBook than they do for the paperback equivalent. Part of this expectation comes because of the success of eBooks. Several well-known authors have produced novellas (i.e. short novels) as eBooks, selling for £2-3 ($2-3 in the US) each, and regularly sell their full-sized novels for £5-7 (or $5-8 in the US) in eBook format.

Consequently, your fiction eBook will sell for less money per copy than a non-fiction book. However, the other side of this is that the market for fiction is larger than non-fiction, so what you lose in earnings per book should be made up by your overall volume of sales.

How much money you can expect to make for each book sold

United States and Canada

List Price (excluding sales tax)	Royalty Rate	Delivery Fee	Estimated Royalty per copy
$0.99	35%	Nil	$0.35
$1.99	35%	Nil	$0.70
$2.99	70%	Typically $0.07	$2.04
$3.99	70%	Typically $0.07	$2.74
$4.99	70%	Typically $0.07	$3.44
$5.99	70%	Typically $0.07	$4.14
$6.99	70%	Typically $0.07	$4.84
$7.99	70%	Typically $0.07	$5.54
$8.99	70%	Typically $0.07	$6.24
$9.99	70%	Typically $0.07	$6.94
$10.99	35%	Nil	$3.85
$11.99	35%	Nil	$4.20
$12.99	35%	Nil	$4.55

List Price	Royalty Rate	Delivery Fee	Estimated Royalty per copy
$13.99	35%	Nil	$4.90
$14.99	35%	Nil	$5.25
$15.99	35%	Nil	$5.60
$16.99	35%	Nil	$5.95
$17.99	35%	Nil	$6.30
$18.99	35%	Nil	$6.65
$19.99	35%	Nil	$7.00
$24.99	35%	Nil	$8.75
$29.99	35%	Nil	$10.50

United Kingdom

List Price (excluding VAT)	Royalty Rate	Delivery Fee	Estimated Royalty per copy
£0.75	35%	Nil	£0.26
£0.99	35%	Nil	£0.35
£1.49	70%	Typically £0.05	£1.01
£1.99	70%	Typically £0.05	£1.36
£2.99	70%	Typically £0.05	£2.06
£3.99	70%	Typically £0.05	£2.76
£4.99	70%	Typically £0.05	£3.46
£5.99	70%	Typically £0.05	£4.16
£6.99	70%	Typically £0.05	£4.86
£7.99	35%	Nil	£2.80
£8.99	35%	Nil	£3.15
£9.99	35%	Nil	£3.50
£10.99	35%	Nil	£3.85
£11.99	35%	Nil	£4.20
£12.99	35%	Nil	£4.55
£13.99	35%	Nil	£4.90
£14.99	35%	Nil	£5.25
£19.99	35%	Nil	£7.00
£24.99	35%	Nil	£8.75
£29.99	35%	Nil	£10.50

In case you are struggling to work out conversion rates, $1 is roughly equivalent to £0.62 and £1 is approximately $1.60.

From these figures, you can see that Amazon makes it much more difficult for you to sell expensive eBooks. If you keep your list price between $2.99 and $9.99 in the United States, and between £1.49 and £6.99 in the United Kingdom, then you can earn a reasonable amount for each copy sold. Sell outside of that price range and you have to sell a lot more copies of your book, or you have to sell your book at a significantly higher price, to earn the same amount of money.

How many books can I expect to sell?

Now there is a question! In response, I have to ask the question "how many books do you sell already?"

If you are selling your eBook alongside your printed book, you will probably start selling 10-20% of your printed volumes in eBook form. As your eBook becomes better known, this figure will increase as your book rises through the eBook sales charts. Remember, Amazon is now saying that they sell more eBooks than they sell paperbacks, so you have the potential to double your existing sales volumes on Amazon with your eBook. If your existing books are not available in other countries, your eBook sales could end up being significantly higher as you tap into those new markets.

If you are not yet a published author, of course, none of that helps you at all. To you, my only response to the above question is "I do not know". It is impossible to say how many you might sell without knowing your subject matter, knowing how good your book is, or the size of the market for your book. For you, the future is in your own hands. It is up to you to market and promote your eBook and make it as accessible as possible. Do not worry; we cover all of that in the next two chapters.

As you can see from the tables, with the margins available from Amazon, you do not need to sell many books in order to provide a worthwhile revenue stream.

You can expect to sell around six to eight times as many eBooks in the United States and Canada as you will in the United Kingdom and Ireland.

Amazon does not disclose sales figures for individual eBooks, but they do provide a sales ranking where you can see how well your eBook is selling, compared to every other eBook they sell. You can find this ranking on the individual book pages within Amazon. The *Amazon Bestsellers Rank* can be found in the Product Details section of all book pages.

The ranking system updates every hour. If you sell five or six eBooks in one hour, your book jumps right up the sales rank. It will then gradually drop back down the charts until other people buy your book. This makes your ranking unpredictable when your book first goes on sale and you are only selling a few books. Later, when your eBook is selling in reasonable numbers, you will normally find your sales ranking is reasonably stable.

From personal experience, I know that if I have an eBook ranked on *Amazon.com* at somewhere around 22,000-26,000, I am selling around 75 eBooks a month in the United States. A similar ranking on the Amazon UK web site equates to sales of around 12-15 eBooks a month. If I have an eBook rated somewhere around the 5,000 mark, I am selling around 500 eBooks a month in the United States and around 75-100 eBooks a month in the United Kingdom.

Chapter 5: A strategy for your eBook

In this guide, we are focusing our initial efforts on producing a Kindle eBook and making this successful. Only then will we look at other eBook formats and other book retailers.

The reasons for this are simple: Amazon provides an unrivalled service for eBook producers and works just as hard to promote independent authors as the major publishers.

Other booksellers are different. Most of them continue to promote eBooks from the same big-name publishers they work with on printed books. Unless you are working with a big publisher, your eBook titles will quite simply get lost if you work with them.

The Kindle is the best selling eBook format available today. Kindle format eBooks can be read on most mobile devices. They are also the easiest eBook format to work with from a technical viewpoint.

Amazon is also the biggest bookseller in the world. More people buy eBooks from Amazon than from any other retailer. If you want a best-selling eBook, you have to have your book selling on Amazon in Kindle format.

I do cover formatting and publishing your book in other formats and selling it through other book retailers, but I purposefully leave that until right near the end of the book.

Chapter 6: Preparing your book for market

The most successful writers lay the foundations for their success before they even put pen to paper. They research the market for their future book and identify their target audience first. They find out what other books are available and try to establish a gap in the market to exploit. They then write the book precisely for the group of people who want their book.

This is not just the case with factual books. Fiction and poetry writers can do this too. If you are writing a science fiction book, for example, you can get in touch with science fiction fans online. Ask them about what they want from science fiction books. If your style of writing is similar to that of a famous author, then try and tap into that same market. Entice future customers with some of your own short stories and build up a following even before you have written your book.

If you have gone as far as writing your book and have not yet identified its market and its potential customers, it is time to take a step back and make sure there is a market for it.

There is an easy way to identify the size of a prospective market. Visit the Amazon website and search for other books that cover a similar subject. On each Amazon book page, there is an Amazon Bestsellers Rank within the Product Details section:

Average Customer Review: ☆☆☆☆☆ ☑ (16 customer reviews)

Amazon Bestsellers Rank: 11,639 in Books (See Top 100 in Books)
        #3 in Books > Scientific, Technical & Medical > Engineering >
        #7 in Books > Scientific, Technical & Medical > Engineering >
        #2 in Books > Science & Nature > Engineering & Technology >

This section allows you to see how well (or how poorly) your competitor's books are selling. You can also discover the sales categories for that book. By clicking on the category titles, you can see similar books that are available.

The bestsellers ranks are updated every hour. When you have a brand new book, your book can zoom straight up the bestsellers list just by selling two or three books in one hour, and then drop back down again. Monitoring the bestsellers lists with brand new titles is a little irrelevant at this stage because the figures can jump around all over the place.

Sales ranks are much more consistent when the book is established. The bestseller figures are then more useful because you can genuinely evaluate how well a book is selling.

Amazon does not divulge sales figures based on bestsellers rank. However, my own experience suggests that a constant rank does relate to an approximate number of monthly sales:

Amazon bestseller rank	US monthly sales	UK monthly sales
100,000	10-20 books	3-4 books
50,000	40-50 books	8-10 books
25,000	75 books	15 books
10,000	250-300 books	50-75 books
5,000	500-600 books	80-100 books

If one competitor's book is not selling well, this does not tell you much. However, if you find that no books in that category are selling well, there may not be a significant market for your book.

If you have already written your book, but you have discovered the marketplace is not that large, you may still choose to publish it. You probably will not make a lot of money from the eBook, but there are reasons to launch an eBook other than money. A terrific book can still buck the trend and become the best-selling book in your category. That can be a worthwhile goal in itself, even if it is not solely measured in monetary terms.

Of course, sales ranks can only tell you what is selling at the moment. Sales ranks cannot tell you what will sell next week, next month, or next year. If you are writing a book on a new subject that has not yet reached the attention of the general public, you could be sitting on a best-seller if that subject becomes topical or newsworthy a few months down the line.

Once your book is ready

You have written your book, you have edited and proof-read the manuscript and it is ready to publish. There is just one more step to carry out before getting your eBook converted into Kindle format and up onto the Amazon websites.

This step is the one that almost every author and small publisher forgets to do. You need to prepare your book for market so that potential customers can easily find, and want to buy, your eBook.

Most authors and small publishers do not even think about this step until they have published their book and it is already online. Unfortunately, that is too late. You do the foundation work for marketing and promotion *before* your book goes on sale, not afterwards.

Skip this step, or leave it until your book is published, and your eBook may never sell. Although there are no guarantees that your book will sell well, if you do prepare your book for the market *now*, you ensure that your book has a chance of getting onto the best-seller lists later.

The 'M' word

Marketing. Why are some authors allergic to that word? Are they scared of it? Do they associate it with underhand selling practices of the past? I am not too sure, but there is no need to be frightened of the 'M' word.

You do not need to be a demanding attention-seeker or to make grandiose claims about what you are doing in order to 'do marketing'. You do not have to pretend to be a celebrity. Good marketing is always honest, open and friendly. You want to attract people towards your book because they like you and are interested in what you write about.

We are all writers. So what could be a better way of marketing than by using our writing skills to attract customers? It is an honest way to promote our books, because it demonstrates our individual writing styles. It is open, because people can see how we communicate. It is friendly, because you are attracting people to your work.

Build a better mousetrap...

Apparently, the world will beat a path to your door if you build a better mousetrap. Unfortunately, this does not work with books.

If people do not know about your eBook, they are not going to buy it. Unless you tell the world about your eBook, it is likely to sink without trace. You know the effort involved in writing a decent book. You owe it to yourself to ensure your book is as successful as possible.

Nobody else knows your books as well as you do. You probably already know who your target audience is. Your next challenge is to find out how to get your eBook in front of those people.

Thankfully, that is not as difficult a task as it may seem. People who read eBooks are already comfortable with using the Internet and will often spend quite some time browsing websites. Therefore, concentrate most of your marketing effort on the Internet.

Check out your competitors

Look at the eBooks sold by your competitors on Amazon. What do you think when you see their Amazon book page. Does the cover look inviting? Does the title and sub-title tell you what the book is about? Is there an informative and compelling description? Are there any reviews? If so, what do the reviewers say about this book?

Ask yourself this question: would you buy this book? If not, why not? If you would, what has convinced you that this book would be worth reading?

Do this with all the best-selling books that cover a similar subject to yours. You will find that all the top books have a clear and compelling message on their Amazon book page, targeted at their audience. They have a smart book cover. They have excellent five star reviews from existing customers.

Now consider how you can beat that with your own Amazon listing. You need a clear, focused message that compels people to find out more. You need to make sure that you present your book better than your competitors presents theirs.

Do not write out your Amazon book description just yet. Just keep these points in your mind whilst you are reading the rest of this chapter and when you do write out your detailed book description later on.

Identifying your "key words"

When you search Google to find something, you type in key words that will help you identify a suitable website. Do you live in Coventry and are you looking for a plumber? Then you will probably type the words COVENTRY PLUMBER into Google.

Key words are short phrases – typically two or three words – that people use to search on Google in order to find something. So ask yourself a question: if you want the world to find your book, what key words would they be using?

Consider what words you would use to find your book. Ask friends and other contacts what words they would use to find your book. With half an hour of work, you can probably come up with a list of six to twelve sets of key words that could describe your eBook.

Bear in mind that your potential customer will probably not be after a book at this stage. They are searching for information. Whether that information is in a book or on a website is probably irrelevant to them. For this reason, the word 'book' should not be one of your key words.

For example, the key words that I would use to describe this book could include:

> eBook Publishing
> Publish eBook
> Selling eBook
> eBook Marketing
> Kindle eBook
> Creating an eBook
> Instructions eBook creation
> Creating eBooks
> Creating eBook
> Making a Kindle book

Do not be put off if you are writing fiction or poetry. Key words are just as applicable to you as they are for factual books. Do you have an adventure novel that takes place in Germany in the middle of the Second World War? Then you can probably come up with lots of key words to attract people searching for information about World War II, or for what life was like in Germany under the Nazis, or for people who want a good, old-fashioned adventure story.

When creating your key words, you do not need to worry about apostrophes and different combinations of upper and lower case letters: the search engines ignore these. Plurals are different words, however, so "eBook" and "eBooks" are two entirely different words in the eyes of Google.

Once you have come up with a list of key words that you think may work for you, it is time to find out how many times Internet users search on those key words in Google.

Thankfully, Google itself makes this easy. Their key word search system not only shows how many people search on your specific key words, it suggests some alternative key words that may perform better.

Visit the website https://adwords.google.com/select/KeywordToolExternal. This site allows you to enter your key words:

Google AdWords

Find keywords
Based on one or both of the following:

Word or phrase (one per line)

```
kindle ebook

creating an ebook

instructions ebook creation

creating ebooks

creating ebook
```

☐ Only show ideas closely related to my search terms ⑦

⊞ Advanced options

    Search

Once you have clicked on the Search button, you will see the results of your key word search:

Keyword	Competition	Global Monthly Searches	Local Monthly Searches	Local Search Trends
kindle ebook		40,500	40,500	
creating an ebook		4,400	4,400	
instructions ebook creation	-	-	-	-
creating ebooks		1,600	1,600	
creating ebook		4,400	4,400	
making a kindle ebook	-	-	-	-
kindle ebooks		60,500	60,500	
kindle ebook reader		9,900	9,900	
ebook creation		2,900	2,900	
free kindle ebooks		22,200	22,200	
kindle ebook format		1,900	1,900	
ebooks		3,350,000	3,350,000	
ebook		9,140,000	9,140,000	
ebook creation software		880	880	
ebook software		74,000	74,000	
ebook reader		673,000	673,000	
free ebooks		1,220,000	1,220,000	
ebook creator		14,800	14,800	

The columns show the following information:

Key words

This lists both key words that you entered yourself, and similar key words that Google thinks may be appropriate.

Competition

This shows how many other websites are also competing for the same key word terms. If there is a lot of competition for that key word combination, you are unlikely to rank high up on a Google search under those terms. Conversely, if there is not a lot of competition for that key word, you are likely to get your book much higher up on a Google search.

Global Monthly Searches

This lists how many people search for the key word each month from around the world.

Local Monthly Searches

The local monthly search lists how many people search for the key word every month from your region. This is not quite so relevant for you, unless you have written a book about a geographical location and most of your customers are likely to come from your local area.

Local Search Trends

This tiny bar chart shows how search results for these key words vary from one month to the next. Some key words work well throughout the year. Others are seasonal.

Your key word objectives

You are searching for key words that describe your book well, where competition is below 50% and global monthly searches are reasonably high.

'Reasonably high' is a relative term. You might see key words where millions of people search on it each month, but unless the term is specific to your subject, skip it. Another set of key words may describe your book perfectly, but only 500 people per month look at it. If there is little or no competition for this second set of key words, it is often better to target the specific key words rather than the vague ones.

There are no hard and fast rules. Trust your intuition – you will probably be right.

It is worth experimenting with different combinations of words and seeing what comes up. For example, when I was searching for different phrases for this book, I found that an average of 2,400 people each month typed in the search phrase *How to publish an eBook*. Competition for this phrase was high: about three quarters the way up the bar graph. However, 9,900 people each month typed in the search phrase *How to make an eBook*, and competition for this phrase was low: about a quarter on the bar graph.

Consequently, if I could make the phrase *How to make an eBook* a key word phrase for my book, not only would I have four times the likelihood of people finding my book, but I would have a much greater opportunity to get to the top of the Google search ranking for that phrase.

I also found that 20,000 *more* people each month searched for *Kindle eBooks* (plural) as opposed to *Kindle eBook* (singular). Competition for both phrases was relatively low.

'Long tail' key words

As well as short key word phrases, it is worth looking for a few 'long tail' key word phrases as well. A long tail key word phrase is a four or five word description that people may use to find your book. For obvious reasons, you will get a lot fewer people looking for these phrases, but the people who are searching for these longer phrases are going to be looking for something far more specific than people with shorter, more general search terms.

Whilst you may get fewer people searching for long tail key word phrases, you are much more likely to be ranked higher in search engines like Google and on Amazon for these key word phrases. That means that people looking for these long tail key words are more likely to find out about your book.

Create a long list of key words

Based on the search terms that I entered, I created a long list of key words for my book. For each term, I noted the number of global monthly searches and the competition for that key word phrase:

Key Word phrase	Average Monthly Searches	Competition
Digital Publishing	33,100	40% competition
eBook Publishing	8,100	90% competition
Publishing eBook	5,400	80% competition
How to make an eBook	9,900	25% competition
eBook Marketing	27,100	15% competition
Kindle eBooks	60,500	30% competition
Make an eBook	18,100	25% competition
eBook Software	74,000	15% competition
eBooks for Kindle	60,500	30% competition
Publishing for Kindle	4,400	25% competition
Convert to Kindle	33,100	10% competition
Market eBook	9,900	15% competition

The next step is to get rid of any key words that have over 40-50% competition. If the competition for those key words is too high, you are unlikely to be ranked high on a Google search on these terms.

In my case, that removes four key words: *eBook Publishing, Publishing eBook, Sell eBook* and *eBook Creator*. No matter, I have plenty left.

The next step is to look through that list and see how well each one fits in with my book. Ask yourself what the searcher is after when they type in these key words into Google.

For example, *Digital Publishing* covers many different areas. It covers eBooks, Print on Demand, brochure printing and short-run printing. How likely is it that someone who is searching for *Digital Publishing* is searching for the information that is in my book? "Not very" is the answer, so out it goes.

The same is true with *Kindle eBooks* and *eBooks for Kindle*. Most people who are searching with these phrases are probably searching for books they can download, and not looking to write and produce an eBook of their own.

eBook Software interests me, because there are obviously many people searching for this and competition is extremely low. I am not going to use that in my book, but I may create a web page somewhere about eBook Software, providing a directory of different software services, a short 'how to' article and a promotion for this book. I am going to file this key word phrase away and come back to it later.

What are people searching for if they type in the key words *Convert to eBook*? I am not sure, so I visit Google to find out. The websites that appear are for readers who want to convert documents for their own e-reader. Interesting, but not necessarily the market I am after. Because the volumes are high and the competition is low, I decide to keep it in my list for now, but I will not make this key word phrase a priority.

eBook Marketing and *Market eBook* are two similar key words, but almost three times as many people look for *eBook Marketing*. Competition for both key words is similar. So out of these two phrases, I am going to focus on *eBook Marketing*.

How to make an eBook and *Make an eBook* are two similar key words, but the latter has almost twice the number of searches. In addition, if I focus on *Make an eBook* then I will pick up many of the *How to make an eBook* searches. The competition for both phrases are the same, so again, I only need to work with one of those phrases.

I am now down to a shortlist of key words:

Key Word phrase	Average Monthly Searches	Competition
eBook Marketing	27,100	15% competition
Make an eBook	18,100	25% competition
Publishing for Kindle	4,400	25% competition
Convert to Kindle	33,100	10% competition

These specific key words may not have the highest number of searches per month, but are terms that are relevant to what I am selling, have a reasonably high volume of monthly traffic and little competition from other websites. If I can make my eBook appear high up on Google web searches when people search with these terms, I should have a reasonable number of sales each month.

Making your key words work for you

Now you have your key words, you need to make them work for you. Sometimes a phrase will jump out of you and hit you between the eyes. If that happens, you may want to change the name of your book to match in that key word phrase. This can work well, but it is not essential.

More importantly, you need to make a description for your book that is around two or three paragraphs long. This description should explain what your book does and must include your key words as Google has shown them.

This is an example of a description that I would use for this book. It incorporates all the key words that I have decided to target (shown in bold text) and promotes the book so that people want to read it:

> Have you ever wanted to **make an eBook**? Do you need to know where to start? Creating an eBook and **publishing for Kindle** and other e-readers is straightforward, fun and profitable, but if you have never done it before, it can also be daunting.

> **Make an eBook** is written by best-selling author, Michael Boxwell. It explains how to publish your eBook from scratch, taking your document, preparing it to **convert to Kindle** and other formats, getting it on sale on Amazon and other mainstream bookstores and ensuring you get a book you can be proud of.

> The handbook then goes on to show how free **eBook marketing** techniques can be used to promote and sell your eBooks around the world.

> If you want to be a successful eBook author with a worldwide following, this step-by-step guide provides the road map to success.

You want to write two or three different versions of this description. Each one should be unique and of varying length. Ideally, you need a version that is just a single paragraph in length, incorporating as many of the key words as possible. It is quite useful to have a version that includes just one key sentence followed by a number of bullet points.

As well as incorporating all your key words, your descriptions need to do an excellent job of convincing people that they want to read your book. The description needs to explain what the reader will get out of reading this book and give them a reason to say "I want this book".

Remember that all successful eBooks have a description that gives a clear and compelling message, targeted at a specific audience. Make your book description the best you can.

Once you have written these descriptions, run the spell checker using both the English (US) and English (UK) dictionaries. Put them away somewhere, come back to them later and read them again. Show them to a friend or colleague and, if necessary, fine-tune them.

These descriptions are going to become your main tools in your marketing toolbox. You are going to use them in the description for your book on Amazon, and when promoting your eBook on every other website.

Your eBook title

Do you have an eBook title in mind? Does your title tell people something about the book? If it does not, think carefully about whether you have the right title. If your book title does not describe the book, you probably have the wrong title.

'Cutesy' titles that intrigue but do not inform are a high-risk game. Of course, there are exceptions. '*What Color is your Parachute?*' has been one of the best selling job seekers manuals for decades, whilst '*Orbiting the Giant Hairball*' has also been an enormous best-seller in business books. Yet these books are the exceptions, not the rule. Both books were marketed by highly talented sales-people who understood the psychology of selling and how to get their books in front of the target market.

Allow me to be blunt: unless you are a renowned marketing genius *and* a salesperson with a track record of closing deals, stay well away from obscure titles. Many books have been completely sunk by a bad title. Do not let yours be one of them.

Of course, an odd or witty title may well be particularly suitable for your book. If your book is about funny poems or stories, for example, then an amusing title will work well. In its own way, your funny title will perfectly describe your book.

In the case of this book, my original working title was *A guide to creating and selling Kindle eBooks*. I am sure you will agree this needed improvement. After looking through my key words, a far better title was obvious: *Make an eBook*.

Just as important as your eBook title is a sub-title. A sub-title allows you to explain a little bit more about what the book is about. Your eBook title grabs the customer's attention. The sub-title draws them in.

My title for this book is not enough to draw people in to buy the book. I have to draw people in and describe the book with a sub-title. *A step-by-step guide to successful eBook Publishing and free eBook Marketing techniques* was the result.

A great technique to draw your potential customer in is to include a promise in your sub-title. Tell the reader what they are going to gain by reading your book. In the case of this book, I am promising to give the reader a step-by-step guide to successfully publish and sell their eBook. If you are writing a murder mystery, your promise could be to provide suspense, fear and excitement.

All books contain a promise. Whether it is to entertain, to excite, to thrill, to inspire or to teach, putting that promise onto the cover of the book dramatically improves your sales.

By the time your potential customer has read both the title and the sub-title, they should know what the book is about and if they want to read it.

Why is this so important? Because your book is amongst a thousand others your potential customer might choose. You have a maximum of five seconds of their attention to tell them why they should pick *your* book.

If you do not have a title or sub-title for your book at this stage, it is time to do some brainstorming. Sit down with a notepad and a pen and just come up with as many ideas as you can.

Here are some pointers to get you started:

- Make both the title and sub-title relevant to the book.
- Keep the title short and snappy.
- The sub-title should be descriptive. It should give the reader a reason to choose your book over every other.
- Go and look at titles for other books of a similar genre to yours for ideas and inspiration (but make sure that the titles that you are investigating are the successful ones that sell!)

Your key words that you chose earlier may well give you some ideas that may work for your title and sub-title.

Do not worry if you cannot come up with a suitable title. This is a common problem. The 'eureka moment' always happens sooner or later. Talk to friends and family and ask them for ideas. Look at your key words and maybe try and find some more. Sit down and start writing lots of different titles and then read them out loud. Sooner or later, you will identify the right title for your book. I will let you into a secret: I could not come up with an appropriate title or sub-title for this book until I had written the whole book and sent it to my editor.

Designing your eBook cover

You now know the final title for your eBook. You know how to identify potential customers. Now it is time to design your eBook cover.

Like it or not, a book is judged by its cover. An eBook is the same. You need a book cover that is attractive and appealing and will grab the attention of your potential customers. It has to be better than any other comparable eBook in your sector.

Your eBook cover needs to look like a 'proper' book cover. Wacky shapes or images do not work and neither do '3D' book covers. You will frighten customers away. Your cover needs to be a portrait rectangle and include the book title, sub title and your name. It should look like it belongs on the cover of a quality book.

An attractive picture on a book cover can work well. A professional layout with smart fonts is imperative. Many book cover designers regard a smiling face looking out from the cover as a particularly good way to get more people looking at your book.

Unlike a printed book, you do not need a high-resolution cover for your eBook. Your eBook cover should be no larger than 1280 pixels deep and no narrower than 500 pixels wide. An ideal size is 960 pixels wide by 1280 pixels deep. This will give your cover a similar profile to a traditional book.

There is one thing to consider with an eBook cover, as opposed to a printed book cover. Often the first time someone sees your book cover, it will be as a tiny thumbnail sized image, viewed on a handheld device such as a Kindle or an iPhone. Your book cover must look respectable when shrunk to a thumbnail image. It must also look acceptable in black and white. In short, an eBook cover is possibly the most complicated type of book cover to design well.

Many writers think they have the creative talent to design a great book cover themselves. This always puzzles me, as they would be the first to say that being able to operate a word processor does not make somebody a writer. Why should they think that the ability to operate a graphics package makes them a good book cover designer?

Unfortunately, many attempts by authors to create their own book cover ends up looking sub-standard. They either look messy, confusing or bland.

Unless you can do an outstanding job of producing your own eBook cover, contract it out to a professional designer. Remember, it is not enough to be *almost* as good as other eBooks in your sector. You have to be better.

If money is tight, visit www.fiverr.com and search for 'book cover'. You will find a number of people, including professional designers, prepared to design a book cover for your eBook for just $5 (just over £3).

As part of the research for this book, I tried it out for myself. I got in touch with four people on the fiverr website and asked them to design an eBook cover for me. In total, it cost me $20. Everyone responded with some excellent draft covers within three days. Here is a selection of the covers I received:

As you can see, none of the options were perfect, but a number of them had potential. Each of the sellers offered to make any minor adjustments to the as part of the original fee.

The end of the book

At the end of all my books, I write a letter. It is a simple letter between my readers and me. I thank them for reading my book, give the reader the chance to find out a little bit more about me and to finish the book on a light note.

The aim of the letter is to make the reader feel good and encourage them to take the next step. In the case of this book, the next step is for the reader to produce an eBook. My letter is a small confidence-booster to encourage my readers to make the leap.

You do not need to write your endnote as a letter, but giving your readers something more can be an excellent idea. For instance, you could write about why you decided to write that particular book, or what inspires you to write. If you have other books with a similar subject, you can mention those.

Alternatively, if your book is one of a set, you could include the first chapter of the next book to encourage people to move on to the next one, followed by a link at the end so people can go straight onto Amazon and buy the book.

Because people can buy eBooks so easily, the potential for an impulse buy is much higher than with a paperback book. If your reader has really enjoyed your book, they could read the next one just by touching a few buttons.

Please do not write a huge chapter of acknowledgements at the end of your book. This will just turn your readers off, just at the point where you want to motivate them further. Whatever you put at the end of the book should be uplifting and finish the book off on a high.

Encouraging your readers to get in touch with you

Your new book should have a section called 'About the Author', either at the beginning or the end of the book. You should include a brief bio and a way for readers to get in touch with you. This can be either an e-mail address, a contact form on your own web site, a Facebook page or via Twitter.

If you make it easy for a reader to get in touch with you or follow you on Twitter, it shows you are an open person with nothing to hide.

If you have other eBooks or printed books on sale, your 'About the Author' page should also include details of these other books. If your readers like your current book, they may want to buy another one.

Some authors have their own website with a questions and answers page. These allow readers to ask the author questions directly about the book. This can work extremely well on many levels: both existing readers and prospective readers can see that you are approachable. This will help your reputation, especially if you are writing a technical manual. You will often see this in customer reviews of your book. If you make yourself open and welcoming, it can pay dividends in book sales. It can also be a lot of fun, and it is lovely when someone gets in touch to say how much they enjoyed your book.

Working out a price

You need to consider the correct sale price for your book. Readers expect eBooks to sell for less than printed books. Their reasoning is understandable: there is no printed book and there is no distribution cost, so the price should be lower.

In the UK, there is an inconsistency with eBooks. Printed books are exempt from Value Added Tax (VAT), whilst eBooks are not. This means that 20% of the sale price of your eBook will be going to the government.

Check out the competition on Amazon and look at the prices of similar books. You do not have to be the cheapest, but if you are planning to sell your eBook for $29.99 and similar eBooks sell for $4.99, you are going to struggle to sell many copies. If your book is going to sell at a premium, you have to give your readers a compelling reason to choose your book over anyone else's.

With my own eBooks, I sell the eBook version for 25-30% less than the printed version. This means that I earn about the same amount of money on the book irrespective of which version I sell. Despite the lower price for the eBook version, I have found that my printed book sales have remained constant. My eBook sales have been additional sales.

Pricing fiction

With fiction, readers have a wide choice available to them. Many well-known authors have novellas (i.e. short novels) available at around £1.99 in the UK and $2.99 in North America, with full-length novels selling from around £4.99/$4.99 and upwards.

You need to ensure that your books are competitively priced. If this is your first fiction eBook and you are not yet a published author, you may even want to consider selling it for £1.49 in the UK and $0.99 in North America and see what happens. Authors who sell their books at this price report they sell around three times as many books at that price compared to selling one at $2.99. Unfortunately, this means you only earn half as much money, but for some authors, the potential to win so many more readers is worth the loss of revenue in the short term. If people like your work, they are much more likely to buy other books from you in the future.

In conclusion

This preparation work is vital. You should now have a fantastic title and sub-title that will encourage potential customers to buy your book. You have an outstanding book cover. You have a price and you have a strategy.

Most importantly of all, you have laid the foundations for your success. Everything you do from now on will build on these foundations and ensure that your eBook has a chance at becoming successful.

Chapter 7: Preparing your eBook

Depending on the format of your book to begin with, preparing your eBook may be either a time consuming business or the click of a few buttons. If you have a carefully formatted book, with multiple columns, lots of diagrams and tables and footnotes, you will have several hours or days of work in order to get everything working. If you have a fairly simply formatted document with no pictures and only rudimentary formatting in place, you might be ready to go in less than half an hour.

This section will tell you what you need to do to your document, so that it is ready to be published.

Starting Point

Before you get to this stage, you should have a document that is proofread, edited, and ready to be unleashed on your unsuspecting public. If your document has not been proofread and edited, do not proceed beyond this point. Unprofessionally edited eBooks damage both your own reputation and the reputation of eBooks in general.

But what if you are writing a niche eBook that does not justify the expense of professional editing? What if you cannot afford to get your book professionally proof-read? Then do the next best thing. Use a professional online grammar checker such as grammarly.com and then ask other authors that you know and trust to read your book for you and give you feedback. The results may not be quite as good as getting your work professionally edited, but in most cases it is certainly a big improvement and is well worth the extra time and effort.

Think global

Your book is going to be available worldwide, not just in one country. If you promote your book via the Internet, most of your sales are likely to come from the United States and Canada. Around 20-25% of your sales will come from the United Kingdom and Ireland.

So consider the needs of an international audience. Remember that some words are spelled differently in different countries: Canada, United States, United Kingdom, Australia and New Zealand may all speak and read English as their first languages, but spellings can differ and synonyms and metaphors can be confusing to people living in other countries.

If you are based in the United Kingdom, set your spell checker to English (US) and check your book. Likewise, if you are based in North America, set your spell checker to English (UK) and do the same. If your word processor highlights spellings that do not work in both versions of English, try to use different words or rephrase the sentences.

It has been said that England and the United States are two countries divided by a common language. This is most certainly true with spelling. Just occasionally, it is simply not possible to find a different word. For example, in this book I use the word *centre* (UK), as opposed to *center* (US) and *license* (US), instead of *licence* (UK).

In this case, some research is required. According to my copy of Webster's American Dictionary, 'centre' is an acceptable way to spell 'center' in North America, although it does note that this is chiefly a British spelling. At the risk of my wonderful American readers howling with rage, I have decided to use the British spelling of this word.

With regards the different spellings of the words 'licence' and 'license', the American spelling is correct in the United Kingdom where it is used as a verb. In other words, a *licence* is the text giving permission for the reader to read my book but not to distribute it, but I can grant a *license* to the reader to read the book but not distribute it. So long as I use the word as a verb, I can correctly spell the word *license* for both countries.

Depending on your point of view, either I have created a book that keeps all my readers happy from all around the world, or I have upset everyone who reads this book, no matter where they live!

Tools for the job

You can edit and prepare your eBook using a standard word processor, such as Microsoft Word or OpenOffice. If using Microsoft Word 2007 or Microsoft Word 2010, you will need to save the file in Microsoft Word 2003 format in order to have it converted to Kindle format.

How to save a document in Microsoft Word 2003 format from Microsoft Word 2007/2010

To save your document in Microsoft Word 2003 format using a later version of Microsoft Word, select *Save As...* then select *Word 97-2003 Document* from the pull down list on the *Save As Type:* options list.

Formatting your book

The layout of an eBook is different to a printed book. You cannot make your eBook look like an exact copy of a printed book because you cannot determine the size of the screen of the e-reader.

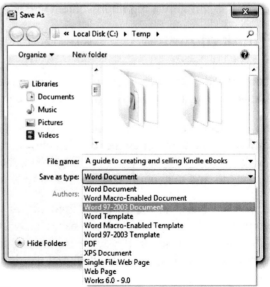

Consequently, you have to simplify the layout of your book and allow the e-reader hardware to format your book to suit its own characteristics and the preferences of the reader.

Many readers choose the size of the fonts they want to read eBooks. In some cases, they can change the font or even adjust the line spacing in order to make the book suit themselves. This means that you have to format your eBook in such a way that it works on lots of different devices, all with different screen sizes and with lots of different font sizes and styles, as decided by the customer.

If most of your book is just text, this is straightforward. If your book includes pictures, diagrams and tables, then you will need to spend a little more time sorting this out.

Columns

All eBooks should display text in a single column on the page. Multiple columns do not present well in an eBook, especially when displayed on a very small screen such as on a mobile phone.

Page Numbers

Your eBook does not require page numbers, as the number of pages the book takes up will be determined on the size of the screen on the e-reader and the size of text the reader wants.

Headers and footers

Your eBook must not have headers or footers.

Text and paragraph formatting

You need to format your text so that it includes almost no formatting at all: choose the font and the spacing between paragraphs, and set the headings to the font and size that you want them. You can use **bold text**, *italics* and <u>underlines</u>, and if you are working with mathematics or scientific equations, you can use superscript and subscript, but then leave everything else alone.

Do not use non-standard fonts. Your book should stick to Times New Roman, Garamond or Arial. Do not adjust kerning or compress or expand a font. Make sure your largest font is no larger than 18 point and that your main body text is presented in 11 or 12-point text.

Set your paragraphs to be left justified. Many e-readers will automatically justify the text anyway, but that is down to the configuration of the e-reader and the preferences of the reader.

Ensure there is a page break before every chapter, but ensure there are no blank lines and no completely blank pages at all in your book.

Line spacing should be set to single.

Each paragraph needs to be separated by either indenting the first line, or by leaving a space between paragraphs (i.e. *block paragraphs*). Typically, indentations are used for fiction and spaces are used for technical books, but you can use either. If you do not format your paragraphs in this way, it becomes much more difficult to see where one paragraph ends and the next starts. This makes your eBook difficult to read.

When setting up paragraph indents and spacing, use the proper tools within your word processor to do these. Do not use tabs or spaces to set up a paragraph indent and never put a hard return (i.e. hit the ENTER key twice) at the end of each paragraph to create a block paragraph.

> Unfortunately, a fault recently appeared on the Amazon document conversion routine with regards to indents. This means that paragraphs formatted using the 'Normal' style will not format with indents correctly when converted to Kindle format. To get around this problem, set up a new style within Word and set up the indents using this new style. You will then find that this works properly when the document is uploaded onto Amazon.

Finally, you cannot use drop caps at the beginning of a chapter with eBooks. If you like your drop caps, some authors format the first letter of a chapter in a larger font size and make it bold. This can be an attractive alternative to drop caps.

If your document includes text boxes, you will need to remove these. You can often use indents instead. Depending on what you are trying to achieve, these will often provide a similar result.

Centre text

If you want to centre text, for example in a headline, create a new text style that centres your text, rather than using the standard centre text option within Word. For some curious reason, the Kindle formatting program ignores text that formatted simply by clicking on the Centre button.

Page breaks

If you have any deliberate page breaks in your book (for instance, between chapters), make sure that you create these new pages by using proper page breaks and not by simply pressing the ENTER key several times.

If you create gaps between your document by pressing the ENTER key multiple times, this can end up creating one or more blank pages inside your eBook when read on an e-reader or mobile phone.

To do a proper page break in Microsoft Word, press and hold down the CTRL button and press ENTER.

Tabs

If you are trying to align your text with tabs, you are asking for trouble with eBooks. Different eBook reading devices format tabs slightly differently and the result can be a mess.

This does not mean that you should use multiple spaces to use the same effect. In fact, this is even worse.

Instead, present the information using a table. Alternatively, create a chart or graph in a graphics package and import it into your document as a picture.

Diagrams, graphics and illustrations

If you have diagrams, tables and illustrations in the book, these should be displayed 'in line' with text, with a line break between them and the text. Illustrations should be high contrast and should not be shrunk down. Remember, the e-reader hardware will scale it to fit its screen.

If you are importing an image into Microsoft Word, trim and crop the image using a proper graphic design package. Do not use the Microsoft Word trimming and cropping tools. These will not work correctly when you export the image to the Kindle eBook format. You should also import the image as a file rather than using the Windows Cut and Paste functions, as these too often cause problems when exporting the image to the Kindle eBook format.

Incidentally, the graphics package you use does not need to be anything particularly special or expensive. All images used in this book have been edited using the *Paint* application built into Microsoft Windows.

If you have technical diagrams, keep them as simple as possible. Remember the size of the diagrams will shrink down to the size of the e-reader display. Consider what they will look like on a mobile phone sized display. If you have complicated diagrams, consider splitting them into two or more smaller diagrams.

All images must be inserted so they are 'in line' with other text. Do not use 'floating' images. These do not reformat well when converted to most eBook formats.

Again, if you are using Microsoft Word, do not use the built in Shapes functionality to create diagrams as these do not always format correctly when exported to the Kindle eBook format. Instead, draw these diagrams in a proper graphics package. Then you can import the images into your document as pictures.

Tables

If your document includes tables, you need to make them as simple as possible. Keep text descriptions short and make sure you have no more than seven columns. If you have any more, the likelihood is that the information will be unreadable on some e-reader systems.

Do not be tempted to reduce font sizes within a table in order to fit in the information you need. Your text may be unreadable on some small-screen devices if you do this.

If you need more than seven columns of data in a table, you need to find a different way to present the data: consider splitting the table into two separate tables, or just find a different way to present the information, such as using a chart or a graph that can be inserted into your document as a graphic.

Footnotes

Use footnotes with care. Footnotes can work well in a printed book, but in an eBook – especially one with a compact display – they can be distracting. If your book does incorporate footnotes as references to other documents, incorporate them as endnotes to be added to a separate reference section at the end of the book.

If your existing book incorporates footnotes, the conversion routine that converts your document into a Kindle eBook will automatically place them as endnotes at the back of your book.

Hyperlinks

If you refer to websites within your book, it is possible to embed these as hyperlinks. Hyperlinks allow you to direct someone to a website simply by clicking on the text. It is entirely up to you if you want to use this feature or not.

If you do use hyperlinks, use them sparingly. If there are many hyperlinks in an eBook, it is too easy to click on a link accidentally. It also looks bad on you if the hyperlink is out of date.

The front of the book

When you pick up a book off the shelf, the front of the book always follows a standard format. You have a page dedicated to the book title and author (and publisher), followed by copyright information.

The same is true with an eBook. You need to include this information in your eBook just as you would with a printed book.

Your title and copyright page must include the following information:

Book Title

Author Name

Copyright *year* Author Name

You may also wish to add more information on your copyright page, such as a hyperlink to your website.

You do not need to include an ISBN number on a Kindle eBook, although many publishers do include them on their eBooks. If your eBook is to have an ISBN number, this should be printed on the title page.

License to Readers

Your license to readers acts as a gentle reminder that the reader has the right to read the book but not to give it away to other people.

Feel free to copy and use the text I use for my eBooks:

> *Whilst we have tried to ensure the accuracy of the contents in this book, the author or publishers cannot be held responsible for any errors or omissions found therein.*
>
> *All rights reserved. This eBook is licensed for your personal use only. This eBook may not be resold or given away to other people. If you are reading this book but did not purchase it, you are requested to buy your own copy. Thank you for respecting the hard work of this author.*

Of course, this assumes that you are selling your book. If you want to give away your eBook free of charge, your text will be different:

> *Thank you for downloading this free eBook. You are welcome to share it with your friends. You may reproduce it, copy it and distribute it for non-commercial purposes, providing the book remains in its complete original form without modification. Thank you for respecting the hard work of this author.*

Contents, Indexes and page numbers

Tables of contents work differently in an eBook compared to a printed book. Instead of page numbers, your contents pages require *hyperlinks* to link to the relevant section of your book. Hyperlinks allow a reader to select the chapter or section from the contents page and jump directly to that section.

If you are using Microsoft Word, it is very easy to configure a table of contents so that it generates hyperlinks and does not generate page numbers.

First of all, create a new Table of Contents by selecting the *Insert Table of Contents* option from the *Table of Contents* menu, as shown in the following picture:

Then untick the *Show Page Numbers* option from the Table of Contents screen (point 1 in the following image), and tick the *Use hyperlinks instead of page numbers* option (point 2 in the following image). Then click on the OK button to create your new table of contents.

Because an eBook is an electronic document, you do not need to provide an index. Your reader can search for a specific word of phrase using the e-reader search facility. Do not put a specific index into your eBook.

If you already have created an index for your eBook, you need to remove both the index and the index entries that are embedded into your text.

To do this, you need to view the hidden index fields within your document. With Word 2007/2010, you can do this easily by clicking on the Show/Hide button on the *Home* menu:

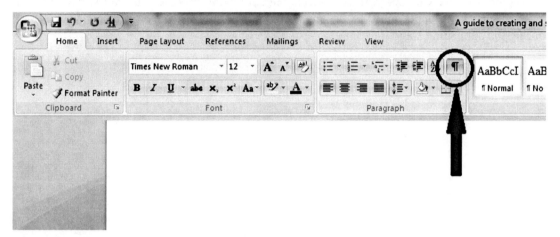

Once you do this, all the hidden formatting codes can be seen in your work. You can see where you have used tabs and carriage returns, and you can find all your index entries, marked like this:

{XE "*index entry*"}

You can then use the Word Search and Replace option to search for {XE and remove each of these manually.

Don't Panic!

If you are not sure whether you have the formatting right in a particular area of your document, make a note of your concern and then move on.

You are unlikely to get everything right the first time. As part of the publishing process, you can preview your eBook and make sure that everything is formatted correctly at that point. You can then pay special attention to the areas you were concerned about to make sure that everything is working correctly.

If you have mistakes, you can then come back to your document and make the changes you need.

In conclusion

Formatting your eBook may be quite time consuming, or it may be quite easy, depending on what you have to start with.

If most of your book is pure text and your original document is not over-formatted, you will probably be able to do everything in half an hour. If your book contains lots of diagrams, pictures or tables, you will need to spend more time fine-tuning your document.

If you are not sure whether you have formatted something correctly, do not worry about it. You will have the opportunity to fix any formatting issues when you preview your eBook during the publishing stage.

Chapter 8: Publishing your eBook on Amazon

This is the exciting bit: it is time to get your eBook converted into Kindle format and on sale at Amazon.

We will be publishing our books directly through Amazon's *Kindle Direct Publishing* system. This system is open to both authors and publishers and gives you the fastest and most profitable route to market.

How Kindle Direct Publishing works

The Kindle Direct Publishing system is straightforward. You upload your eBooks and provide a description and price. You specify whether you want *Digital Rights Management* (DRM) enabled and whether you are happy for Kindle readers to lend your eBook to their friends. Once the eBook has been verified and approved by Amazon, your book goes on sale on to all Amazon sites around the world.

At any time, you can check your sales on the Kindle Direct Publishing website and Amazon keeps track of all revenue. Amazon pays you your royalties sixty days after the end of the calendar month during which the sales occur.

Registering for a Kindle Direct Publishing account

First, you will need a new account on Amazon. If you are an Amazon customer, you probably already have an account. However, it is a good idea to have a separate account for publishing and promoting your own books.

To create your new Amazon account and gain access to the Kindle Direct Publishing system, go to the following website:

kdp.amazon.com

Registering takes just a few minutes. As well as entering your personal details, you will need to enter details for payment, so that you can receive royalty payments from Amazon.

Once you are up and running, take a few minutes to explore the website. There is lots of online help and a support forum available, plus sales reporting tools so you can see how many eBooks you have sold once you are up and running.

Publishing your book

Go to the bookshelf page on the Kindle Direct Publishing website, by clicking on the *bookshelf* option at the top of the screen (step 1 below):

Next, click on the *Add a new title* button (step 2 above).

You will now go to a new screen that will ask you to enter the details for your new book:

Book Basics

Title:

New Title 1

☐ This book is part of a series (What's this?)

Series title: Volume:

Edition number (optional): (What's this?)

Description: (What's this?)

4000 characters left

Book contributors: (What's this?)

[Add contributors]

Publishing Details

Language: (What's this?)   Publication date (optional):

<Select language> ▼

Publisher (optional): (What's this?)   ISBN (optional): (What's this?)

Publishing Rights

Publishing rights status: (What's this?)

○ This is a public domain work.

FAQs

Who are contributors?
Contributors include the author(s) and individuals who created or editing the content — authors, editors, illustrators, translators, and more. At least one author name is required.

Should I use my physical book's ISBN?
Provide us with an ISBN that is exclusive to the digital content you are uploading. ISBNs assigned to the physical editions should not be used, as they are unique to that edition.

What are browse categories and search keywords?
Selecting browse categories will allow you to place a title among books of a similar genre. Providing search keywords will expand the set of terms that your title is searchable by in the Kindle Store. You can choose up to two browse categories and enter multiple search keywords.

Should I enable Digital Rights Management?
Digital Rights Management (DRM) is intended to inhibit unauthorized access to or copying of the content you upload. DRM is a one-time option and cannot be changed once selected.

○ This is not a public domain work and I hold the necessary publishing rights.

Browse and Search

Categories:

[Add categories]

Search keywords (optional): (What's this?)

[   ]

Product Image

Upload image (optional):

No image available
Upload your image

This image will appear in search results and on the product detail page for your content. If you do not upload an image, a placeholder image will be used. You can upload your image to override the placeholder image at any time.
(Example placeholder image)

> Product Image Guidelines

[Browse for image...]

Book Content

Select a digital rights management (DRM) option: (What's this?)

○ Enable digital rights management

○ Do not enable digital rights management

Book content file:

[   ]   [Browse for book...]

> Help with formatting   [Upload book]

<< Back to Your Bookshelf   [**Save and Continue**]   [**Save as draft**]

The page is reasonably self-explanatory. There are useful help prompts on the right hand side of the screen. If you are stuck at any stage, you can click on the *(What's this?)* prompts next to the titles to find out more information.

A few specific pointers to some of the options on this screen that may require a little more explanation:

Title

You should include both your main title and your sub-title in the Title field, separating the sub-title from the title with a hyphen.

Series Title and Volume

If your eBook is one of a series, you should provide the full series title and volume name (or number) here. This ensures that when prospective buyers find your book on Amazon, they can see information about all the other eBooks in the same series.

Edition Number

If your eBook is updated every year, or if it is an updated version of a previous release, you can put the edition number or year here.

Description

It is important to get your description right. Use the best description from your choice of three or four that you have written and paste it into this field.

Amazon is going to use this description to promote your eBook. It is the most important single thing to get right on your Amazon listing.

Book Contributors

You must include at least one book contributor to your eBook. A book contributor can be the author, an illustrator, an editor, a translator or anyone else that you would like to acknowledge as a contributor to your book.

Publishing Details

You must specify a language for your book, but all the other options under publishing details are optional.

You should enter a publication date. It shows your book to be a new title and some people will look at your book for that reason alone.

Because your eBook is only going to sell on Amazon, you do not need an ISBN number. However, if you have access to ISBN numbers, it can be worth using one. It demonstrates to both Amazon and your customers that you are a serious writer.

Your ISBN number must be a unique number for this edition of the book. If you have previously had this book published in another form, or using a different eBook provider, you **cannot** use that ISBN number to describe this book. If you do enter an ISBN number that is already in use, you are likely to cause significant cataloguing problems, which may disrupt book sales of both your titles on Amazon. You are also likely to have your eBook removed from Amazon. If in doubt, leave it out.

Categories

Categories are one of two ways that Amazon catalogues your eBook. It is worth spending a few minutes looking at all the categories that are available to you and making sure that your eBook is listed in the right ones.

Check your direct competition and make sure that you are in the same categories as the best selling books. When a potential customer is looking at the other book, they are more likely to find yours as an alternative if you use the same categories.

You can specify up to two categories for your book. Of course, you can choose to leave your eBook uncategorized. However, if you do this you are making it much harder for your potential customers to find your eBook.

Product Image

The Product Image is your eBook cover. We have already discussed the importance of having a good cover earlier in the book. Whilst Amazon does not insist that you upload a product image, your eBook faces a much greater struggle if you do not have one.

Book Content

Under the Book Content section, you first need to specify a Digital Rights Management (DRM) option.

To recap, Digital Rights Management allows you to stop people copying of your eBook.

Without DRM, there is the risk that people may start distributing your titles illegally. With my books, I enable DRM for my most important works but do not enable DRM for eBooks that are re-released versions of books that have gone out of print.

Personally, I have seen very little difference in sales on Kindle between DRM enabled books and non-DRM enabled books. My personal preference is to enable DRM on all my Kindle titles.

Once you have specified whether you want Digital Rights Management or not, you can then upload your book content file. This is the document that you have carefully edited and formatted.

Click on the *Browse for book...* button and then select your document to upload. Then click on the *Upload Book* button.

At this point, the system will upload your file and then convert it to Kindle format. Depending on the size of your file and the speed of your Internet connection, this may take several minutes.

Despite the message saying that you can continue with the upload process whilst the processing takes place, it is best to let the Amazon conversion complete. Once it is uploaded, you then get a new option appear on the screen:

Previewing your book

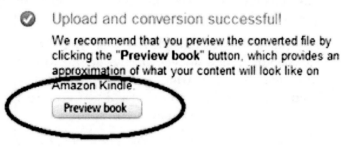

Previewing your book is a vital step. You need to check that the book is laid out as you would expect when viewed on a Kindle e-reader.

When you click on the *Preview book* button, a virtual Kindle e-reader will be shown on the screen, showing your book. Left and right arrows are shown at the top of the screen to allow you to turn the pages. At the bottom, you can see which location you are at within the book. You can also adjust the font size, so you can see what the book looks like with larger or smaller text.

◀ ▶   Download HTML (Whats this?)

yourself and then explains the technicalities of producing an eBook and getting it on sale.

Finally, and probably most importantly of all, the guide suggests some simple, low cost steps that you can take to promote your eBook and get it noticed by your prospective customers.

What this guide does not cover

This guide does not tell you how to write, proof-read or edit a book. All these are very necessary and vital steps for producing any polished work and if your work has not been professionally proof-read and edited, then it is not ready to be released as an eBook.

The guide also does not tell you what you should write about or how to get started in the writing profession. It starts from the point where you already have a completed book and you are ready to create an eBook version to put on sale.

This guide also assumes that you know how to use

Location: 10354   of 94430   Font size: 3 ▼   (Menu ▲)

The location number at the bottom of the screen may look a bit odd at first. Instead of showing page numbers, which can change depending on whether you make the text large or small, it shows your location in terms of how many characters you are into your text.

You need to check the layout of your entire eBook using this preview facility. Pay particular notice to the cover, index pages, chapter headings, section headings and any photographs, tables, drawings or diagrams that you have in the book. Make sure there are no blank pages at the start of the book and make sure the layout still works if you zoom the font size up to the biggest size and reduce it to the smallest.

Normally something does not look quite right on your first attempt. If this happens, simply open up the document in your word processor and make the changes you want. Then save the file, upload it and check it on the preview function again.

Whatever you do, do not rush this stage. The quality of your book depends on getting this step right. Take your time and make sure you make the layout of your eBook as good as it can be.

Sometimes this means suspending the upload onto Amazon and going back to spend a lot of time on reformatting something such as a diagram or a table. In that case, Amazon gives you the option to save everything as a draft and come back to it later.

Once you are happy with the layout of your new eBook, you can go to the next step. Close down the Kindle Preview screen and then click on the *Save and Continue* button. You are now at the 'Rights and Pricing' screen:

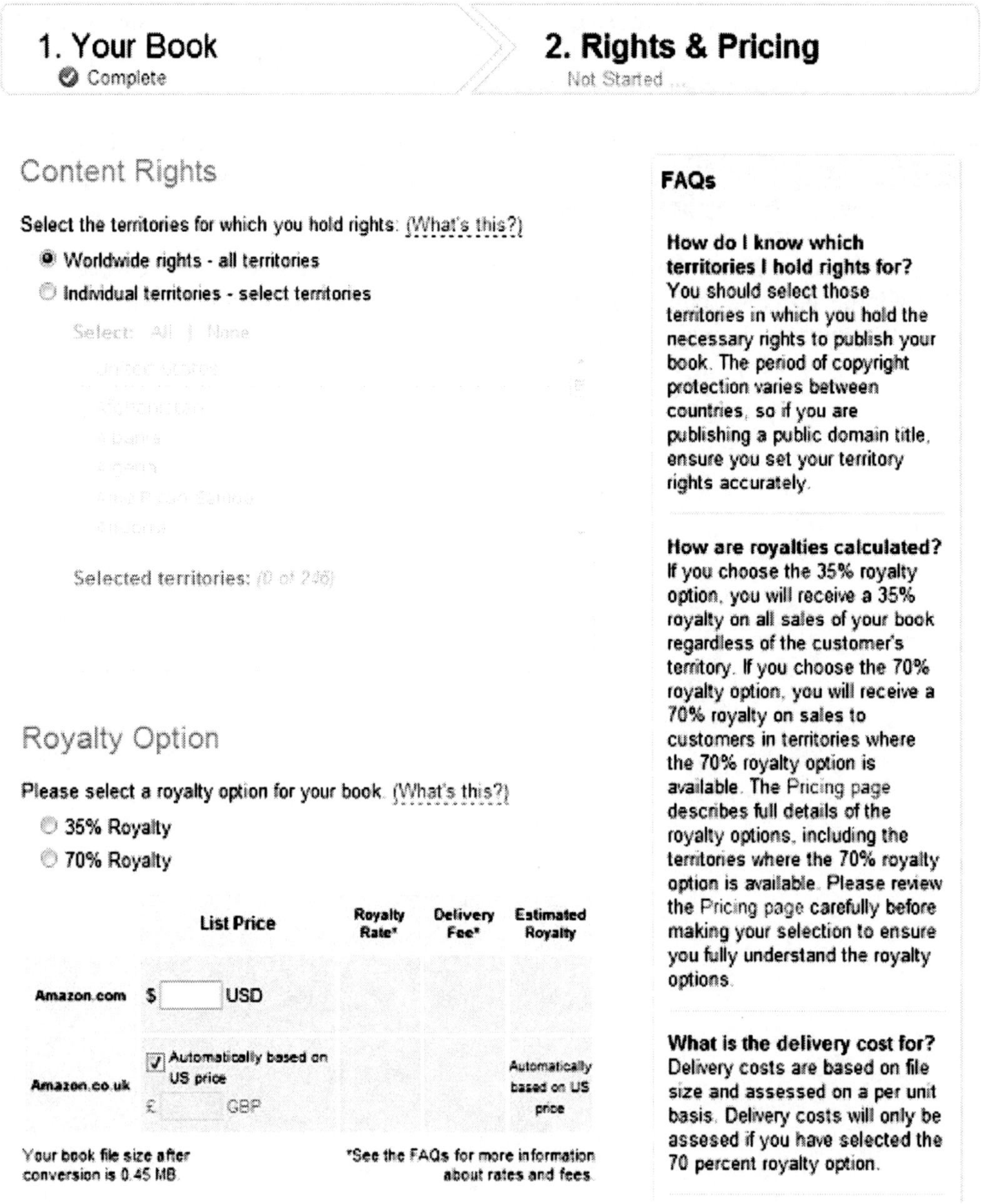

1. Your Book	2. Rights & Pricing
✓ Complete	Not Started ...

Content Rights

Select the territories for which you hold rights: (What's this?)

- ● Worldwide rights - all territories
- ○ Individual territories - select territories

  Select: All | None

  [territory list illegible]

  Selected territories: (0 of 246)

Royalty Option

Please select a royalty option for your book. (What's this?)

- ○ 35% Royalty
- ○ 70% Royalty

	List Price	Royalty Rate*	Delivery Fee*	Estimated Royalty
Amazon.com	$ [____] USD			
Amazon.co.uk	☑ Automatically based on US price £ [____] GBP			Automatically based on US price

Your book file size after conversion is 0.45 MB

*See the FAQs for more information about rates and fees

FAQs

How do I know which territories I hold rights for?
You should select those territories in which you hold the necessary rights to publish your book. The period of copyright protection varies between countries, so if you are publishing a public domain title, ensure you set your territory rights accurately.

How are royalties calculated?
If you choose the 35% royalty option, you will receive a 35% royalty on all sales of your book regardless of the customer's territory. If you choose the 70% royalty option, you will receive a 70% royalty on sales to customers in territories where the 70% royalty option is available. The Pricing page describes full details of the royalty options, including the territories where the 70% royalty option is available. Please review the Pricing page carefully before making your selection to ensure you fully understand the royalty options.

What is the delivery cost for?
Delivery costs are based on file size and assessed on a per unit basis. Delivery costs will only be assesed if you have selected the 70 percent royalty option.

Kindle Book Lending

☑ Allow lending for this book (Details)

What is Kindle Book Lending?
The Kindle Book Lending feature will allow users to lend digital books they have purchased through the Kindle Store to their friends and family. Each book may be lent once for a duration of 14 days and will not be readable by the lender during the loan period. All KDP titles are enrolled in lending by default. For titles in the 35% royalty option, you may choose to opt out of lending by deselecting the checkbox under 'Kindle Book Lending,' but you may not choose to opt out a title if it is included in the lending program of another sales or distribution channel. For more details, see section 5.2.2 of the Terms and Conditions.

☐ By clicking Save and Publish below, I confirm that I have all rights necessary to make the content I am uploading available for marketing, distribution and sale in each territory I have indicated above, and that I am in compliance with the KDP Terms and Conditions.

<< **Back to Your Bookshelf**　　　　　　[**Save and Publish**]　[**Save for later**]

Let us look at this screen in more detail.

Content Rights

You can specify which countries you want to sell your eBook in by configuring the Content Rights.

If you have written your book yourself, you automatically have worldwide copyright on your book. Unless you have very good reason not to sell it worldwide, you should select this option.

If you are republishing someone else's book and you only have the rights to sell it in a particular country, then you need to specify the individual territories in which your eBook can be sold.

Unless you have a specific reason not to sell your book worldwide, it is worthwhile telling Amazon that you have worldwide rights. This gives you the opportunity to sell books all around the world.

If you are based in the United Kingdom, this gives you access to the lucrative North American market, giving you the opportunity to sell to a marketplace that is roughly eight times the size of the domestic market. North America writers also gain access to Europe, with the potential to increase your sales by around 10-15% at no extra cost to yourself.

Royalty Options

Amazon offers two different royalty options on eBooks. These are likely to change from time to time, so check the Amazon Kindle Publishing website to find the latest options.

Today, the standard royalty is 35% of the list price. With this option, Amazon allows you to set whatever list price you like. They can offer the book at a discount should they wish, but they will always pay you 35% of your list price.

The second royalty option is 70% of the sale price. With this option, Amazon allows you to set a list price between $2.99 and $9.99 in the United States and between £1.49 and £6.99 in the United Kingdom. They charge you a small delivery fee, which is based on the size of your book in megabytes, which is deducted from the royalty. They also reserve the right to offer the book at a discount should they wish, and you will then receive a 70% royalty based on this sale price.

This 70% royalty option is a very good deal. When Amazon buy printed paperback books from publishers, they are used to having between 50-65% discounts from list price. For eBooks, Amazon is accepting only 30% discount. The additional delivery fee they charge is tiny, typically equating to around 5-15 cents (3-10 pence) for most books. It is not a big price to pay to get your eBooks up on sale at the biggest bookshop in the world.

Royalty Option

Please select a royalty option for your book. (What's this?)

○ 35% Royalty
● 70% Royalty

	List Price	Royalty Rate*	Delivery Fee*	Estimated Royalty
Amazon.com	$ 9.99 USD	35%	n/a	$3.50
	Must be between $2.99 and $9.99	70%	$0.07	$6.94
	☐ Automatically based on US price			
Amazon.co.uk	£ 6.99 GBP	70%	£0.05	£4.86
	Must be between £1.49 and £6.99			

Your book file size after conversion is 0.45 MB.

*See the FAQs for more information about rates and fees.

It is worth playing about with different figures on the royalty options and list price to see what they look like. The UK list price can be automatically calculated based on the US price, or you can set different prices for each country automatically.

Royalty Option

Please select a royalty option for your book (What's this?)

- 35% Royalty
- 70% Royalty

	List Price	Royalty Rate*	Delivery Fee*	Estimated Royalty
Amazon.com	$ 12.99 USD Must be between $0.99 and $200	35%	n/a	$4.55
Amazon.co.uk	☐ Automatically based on US price £ 9.99 GBP Must be between £0.75 and £120	35%	n/a	£3.50

Your book file size after conversion is 0.45 MB.

*See the FAQs for more information about rates and fees.

Once you have finished setting the prices, you are ready to go. Tick the box to confirm that you have the copyright to your book and that you agree with the terms and conditions. Then click on the SAVE AND PUBLISH button.

Once you have done this, you will be taken to the BOOKSHELF page on the Kindle Direct Publishing website. You will be able to see your book listed there, with the status of 'TO BE REVIEWED'. Amazon reviews every book to ensure that it conforms to the Kindle Terms and Conditions. This process can take two to three days to complete, but I have never known a book be refused unless there are problems with the formatting of the book.

If this happens, you will be contacted by a member of Amazon explaining what the problem is with the book. You then need to rectify the faults and resubmit it.

That is it. Now be patient for a couple of days and keep checking the site. In the meantime, it is time to start planning your book promotions and telling the world about your exciting new book. We will cover that in the next chapter.

Chapter 9: Promoting your eBook

Welcome to the unlimited bookshop

Imagine a bookshop where every book that has ever been printed is available for you to buy. A bookshop where no book is ever out of stock. A bookshop where your books can be sold year in and year out and get equal storefront space to all the latest titles. Welcome to the world of the eBook.

In the printed book world, books have a shelf life of just a few months before they end up on the remaindered shelves. Big publishers spend a fortune to promote their books in the first few weeks to ensure they sell immediately. It is 'big bang' marketing and very effective in a retail environment. Small publishers and independent authors do not have the money to make their mark and struggle to make an impact.

eBooks change the game. With eBooks, your book can be on sale for years, so you can play the long game with sales and book promotion. Long after the big publishers have forgotten about their last big seller, you can be continuing to grow your sales with your eBook.

Fancy outselling Dan Brown? Well, I have some good news. You might not be able to outsell his book in the first few months of his launch, but in the long term, your eBooks could start ranking higher than his in the sales charts.

Major publishers promote their big name authors for the first few weeks and then stop. As their publicity dries up and you continue with your promotion, your eBooks start slowly climbing up through the charts, whilst the big name author's books drop off.

If you do not believe me, go and look at the sales ranks for the Kindle edition of my *Solar Electricity Handbook*. Then compare it to the sales rank for *Angels and Demons* or *Deception Point*. The eBook editions of all three books were released at around the same time, yet my book is usually outselling his.

How is this possible? I have played the long game. Dan Brown's publishers went for the short-term sale. Overall, I might not have made as much money on my books as Dan Brown has on his, but this year, next year and the year after, I will probably make more money on my older eBook titles than he does on his.

The first rule of promotion: do not give up

Promotion and marketing is a funny old game. Much of the time when you are working on promoting your eBook, you do not know whether you are wasting your time or whether you are on the verge of breaking into the big time. Quite often, effort that you put in now will only start paying back in two or three months time: you suddenly get a surge in book sales and you have no idea why it has happened.

Sometimes, it can seem quite dispiriting. Starting out with a new book and telling the world about it can feel like the most difficult job in the world. It is easy to get discouraged if you have spent huge amounts of time promoting your book and at the end of the week, only two people have bought copies.

There is a golden rule in marketing. Never give up. Most authors, like most small businesses, give up marketing their product as a lost cause far too quickly. If you get the foundations in place to make your book successful, expect it to take between three and six months for your book to start selling in reasonable numbers.

It will take you at least three or four days of hard work to get your promotion set up, and then at least half an hour a week for the next six months to make it successful and keep it at the top. Even that is no guarantee of success, but if you want your eBook to have a chance to make it big, you are going to need to put in the effort.

Put together a plan

You can promote a book in many ways. Do not attempt to do everything in one go. You will rush it and not do a good job, or you will just burn yourself out. You need to write out a marketing plan with a list of everything you are going to do. Then simply work through the list, ticking off each task as you complete them.

You will need to schedule some time. Some people prefer to devote a few days to focus on marketing at the start. Others like a 'little and often' approach. It is your decision as to which you choose.

Once you have built up some momentum, make sure that you spend at least half an hour each week doing something to promote your eBook. If you can spare more time, so much the better, but half an hour of concentrated effort is better than a couple of hours of unstructured waffle.

So read this chapter a couple of times. Give it some thought. Then write yourself a plan of action.

Promoting your book for the long-term

It is a common complaint amongst authors that when they stop actively promoting their books, sales dry up completely.

This actually says more about how the authors are promoting their books than about marketing and book sales in general: if you get a mention in a newspaper or a magazine, or an interview on local radio, you might get two or three days of good sales, but after that, sales dry up again. It is the same with a book signing: you get one day of good sales, but then very little afterwards.

Whilst all these activities can be useful, what is needed is a promotional campaign that works in the long term. This takes just as much dedication, effort and commitment as any other form of book promotion, but has the benefit of continuing sales for months and years after the initial effort was made.

This form of promotion has a different effect than traditional book promotion methods. With traditional book promotion methods, you get a spike in sales and then they quickly drop away again. With longer-term promotions, you often do not get the initial spike. Instead, you get a gradual flow of sales over a period of months, or even years, before they gradually fade away again.

With this second method, if you stop promoting your book for a few weeks or months, you should continue to get sales. Eventually, if you stop promoting your book completely, the sales will die away, but so long as you continue to put a little effort into marketing your book, you could well continue to see income from your book for a number of years.

Finding your audience

Because we want long-term results, we will focus most of the promotion work on the Internet.

We will not completely ignore newspapers, magazines, and more traditional ways of book promotion, because they do have their place. However, some newspapers and magazines who will happily review printed work tend to ignore eBooks unless you are a well-known author.

People who buy eBooks are confident in using technology and tend to use the Internet a lot. Therefore, promoting your eBook via the Internet gives your book the best exposure to your customer base.

It's all about key words, stupid!

Thankfully, you have done a lot of the work already. If you have found a good set of key words, then you have a good chance of getting your books found. Your next step is to make sure that you use these key words every time you promote your eBook on the Internet.

You should have at least three versions of your eBook description, of varying length and presenting the information in different ways. Do not be afraid to add more versions of your description either. The more versions of your eBook description you have, the more successful you will be in regularly appearing at the top of Google searches.

Promoting your new eBook on Amazon

Kindle books sell on the various Amazon websites across the world. Amazon actively promotes their company in the United States of America, Canada, the United Kingdom, Ireland, Germany, France and Japan.

Fortunately, Amazon provides an excellent set of tools in order to help you promote your eBooks. You can create detailed book descriptions, provide key word search 'tags' and even add videos and photographs to your book page.

You can also promote yourself with your own author's page, providing more detail about yourself and your work.

Improve your product listing

You will have already got your product description onto your product page on Amazon. There are a few things to do in order to improve your listing.

Start by going to your product page and scrolling down to the *Tag This Product* section. Tags in Amazon are a way of posting your key words onto your eBook. You can include as many tags as you like. These tags help people find your eBook. Amazon also use these tags to suggest your eBook as an alternative to other books that people may be looking at whilst searching the Amazon website.

Tag this product (What's this?)
Think of a tag as a keyword or label you consider is strongly related to this product
Tags will help all customers organize and find favorite items.

Your tags: [_____] (Add)

(Press the 'T' key twice to quickly access the "Tag this product" window.)

To add your key words to your eBook, type in each key word phrase and click on the *Add* button. Do this for every key word phrase in your list.

Add more photographs

At the top of your listing, underneath the photograph of your book, there is an option to share your own customer images. Using this feature, you can add additional photographs about the book. You can include photographs of you as the author, or of illustrations or diagrams within the book. In fact, it can be of whatever you want.

Probably only ten percent of people will bother to check these additional photographs, but if it encourages those ten percent to go ahead and buy your eBook, it is worth doing.

Get yourself an Amazon author's page

Amazon loves authors. In fact, Amazon loves authors more than they love publishers. If you are an author, you can access some great extra features.

Amazon's main hub for authors is called *Author Central* and it can be accessed at the web address authorcentral.amazon.com. It is a very powerful tool that Amazon provides that allows you to track your sales, monitor the performance of your books and gain access to the Amazon Help Desks. It is also a very powerful tool for promoting your books and eBooks.

If you do not yet have an Author Central account, join up. It is free and takes only a few minutes. Upload a photograph of yourself, update your biography and make sure your eBooks are linked through to your author central profile.

If you want, you can also upload a video. This can be a video to promote your eBook, a video interview, a book signing video, or anything else that you like the idea of trying.

Once you have linked your books on Author Central, the Amazon web page for your book will also include links through to your author central profile. It all helps build your credibility as a professional author.

Linking your books

If your eBook is a new version of an existing book, you can ask Amazon to link the listings. This has the benefit of linking across your reviews between both books and allows Amazon to show them as two different versions of the same book.

If someone finds your eBook but wants a printed book, having the books linked means that person can easily buy the printed book. Likewise, if someone wants an eBook and finds your printed book on Amazon, they can easily buy the eBook version.

To link your books, you need to get in touch with Amazon Customer Service and ask them to link the two titles together. You do this through the customer services contact on the Amazon web site.

This is the web address to contact customer services in the United States and Canada:

www.amazon.com/gp/help/contact-us/general-questions.html

This is the web address for the United Kingdom and Ireland:

www.amazon.co.uk/gp/help/contact-us/general-questions.html

Provide the title, the ISBN number of your printed book and the unique ASIN reference number or your ISBN number for your Kindle book (you can find the ASIN number in the Product Details section on the Amazon page for your eBook). Explain that you want to link the two titles together. If the two books have the same title, your books should be linked together without a problem.

It usually takes a few days for your books to be linked. Make sure that the books are linked on both the US web site and the UK web site. Just occasionally, they will end up being linked on one but not the other. If that happens, contact customer services in the country where the two books are not linked and ask again.

Get yourself some early reviews

Nothing sells books and eBooks as much as five star reviews. Nothing sinks a book quite so quickly as lots of bad reviews. Therefore, you need to get some good reviews for yourself.

You must avoid two things with reviews. Firstly, do not make up your own reviews. This is blatant cheating, and you would be surprised on how quickly you will be found out. If that happens, you will then get some very negative reviews and comments from other people. Trust me, creating your own reviews is dishonest and will backfire on you.

The second thing to avoid is asking your friends and family to write a review, unless they have read your eBook first. Reviews that have been written by friends who have not read the book themselves come across as false and again, can backfire on you.

Instead, talk to people who are genuinely interested in your book and ask them if they would read it and provide you with honest feedback. These can be friends and family. They can also be other authors that you have met through a writers group or convention.

If your contacts like your book, ask them if they would be prepared to post their reviews on Amazon. If you know these contacts well, ask them if they would be willing to post their reviews on the UK, US and Canadian websites. This way, you are getting the reviews you need to encourage other people to buy your book. At the same time, your potential customers are getting honest feedback from other people who are genuinely interested in your subject material.

Get yourself an Amazon Associate account

We have not quite finished with Amazon yet. Sign up for an *Amazon Associate* account. The Amazon Associate scheme allows you to place a link for your eBook on your website (or anyone else's for that matter) and earn a commission if someone buys your book. Even better, if someone clicks on a link you have posted on your website but then buys something else entirely, Amazon also pays you a commission on that.

As we will see later on, the Amazon Associate scheme is a fantastic system for promoting your book as it provides an incentive for other website owners to promote your eBook on your behalf.

Get yourself a video

Get yourself a video of your book. Whether it is an out-and-out advertisement for your book, or you reading an excerpt of your book, interspersed with a few photographs, a YouTube video can be picked up by lots of people.

Your video does not have to be long – in fact, short 30-50 second videos can often be the best, as they will grab people's attention.

When creating a video, make sure it is easy for people to find out where they can get your book. Repeat the title of the book at the end of the video and explain that it is available on Kindle from Amazon.

Fiverr.com

Would you rather not record yourself? Perhaps you are not sure how to do it, or just feel nervous in front of a camera? Here is a solution. Get someone else to do it for you and pay them five dollars.

Five dollars for a video? Absolutely. A new phenomenon on the world wide web is a website called Fiverr.com. Entitled "the place for people to share things they're willing to do for five dollars", the site is full of people offering all sorts of products and services for $5.

Some of the most impressive are the videos. Professional and semi-professional presenters are prepared to record themselves reading an excerpt from your book on camera, edit it and provide you with a complete video ready to go... for just $5. Other people are offering high tech video introductions designed to grab your viewer's attention. The choice is endless. Visit www.fiverr.com and see for yourself.

What to do with your video

Once you have your video, post it up on YouTube, post links to it on Facebook and Twitter. When you post up the video on YouTube, you will be asked to enter key words. Include all your key words so that the video can be picked up easily.

The more people who see your video, the more people are likely to buy your eBook.

Allow people to read the first chapter of your book for free

One of the most important things you can do to promote your sales is allow people to read the first chapter or two of your book for free. This is the online equivalent of browsing books in a bookshop and definitely encourages people to go ahead and buy your book.

Format your book to look smart, incorporating the cover picture on the first page of the document. Include links at the end of the sample chapter so that people can find out where they can buy the whole book.

Then upload it onto a book browsing website such as SCRIBD.com, ISSUU.com or myEbook.com.

On your website

I assume you already have a website. If not, you should have. Every author ought to have a website where readers can find out more about them and their work.

You may even have a website about your book. This is becoming increasingly popular and can pay dividends. You can include sample chapters from your book, explain more about the book, add some additional content that is not included in your book and get people excited about reading more of your work.

Explaining how to create your own website for your book is really beyond the remit for this book, but if you are a newcomer to creating websites, start with a template such as a Wordpress website (search Google for 'wordpress') or work with a site such as Blogger (www.blogger.com) to create yourself a free website.

Whether or not you have a specific website for your eBook or just have an author's website, it is important that your eBook has a 'home' on the Internet. Create at least one page about your new book. Write a unique description about your book – i.e. one that you are not planning to use elsewhere. Ideally, each page should be around 400-500 words long and must include all your key words.

Ideally, you want more than one page for your book. It can be a good idea to have one page for each of your key word phrases, with each page promoting a different aspect of the book. This can work extremely well for non-fiction books where you are discussing specialist subjects. It shows your readers that you have a depth of knowledge, and will help your Google search rankings on your specialist subject.

It can also work well for fiction books as well: you can have a page on what inspired you to write your book, or how you discovered the characters that make up your book. Anything that inspires the reader to find out more and helps Google 'find' your site.

Include your video on your website. Some people may not be interested in reading your description, but may well be interested in watching your video.

Make sure your web site does a good job of selling your book. Give people compelling reasons for wanting to read it. Provide a link so prospective customers can read the first two chapters free of charge online. Tell them what they will gain from reading your book. Include customer testimonies, and at the bottom of each page, tell them how they can buy a copy of your book. Make it easy for them to say "yes please".

Put a link to your book on Amazon using your Amazon Associates account. This way, people can easily buy your book. You also make an extra commission on every book you sell.

Finally, encourage your readers to get in touch with you, either through a 'contact the author' form or by posting an e-mail address on your site. Potential customers will like the fact you are open and are more likely to buy your eBook.

A book-specific website

If you are writing a series of books, or a book about a specific topic, it really can work well to create a book-specific website: a site that allows you to *give more* to your readers.

If you are writing a non-fiction book, a book-specific web site allows you to add credibility to your book. For instance, the Make an eBook website (www.MakeAnEbook.org) incorporates lots of 'how to' articles, links to a Web TV series on eBook publishing and marketing, an eBook directory and information to eBook readers on how to download software to read eBooks using a variety of devices. The site also allows people to get in touch with me if they have any questions. In short, the site establishes my credentials and encourages people to buy my books, whilst providing useful information for existing readers wanting to find out more.

For works of fiction, a book-specific website allows you to tell people more about the story. You could include additional short stories about some of the characters in your book, anything that both encourages new readers to buy your book and existing readers to find out about other books in the same series.

Your own blog

It's become fashionable for authors to have blogs. So many marketing experts have said for so long that blogs are a vital marketing tool that many authors rush into creating their own blogs and never really think about who their audience is or why they are doing it.

The result is often blogs that are poorly laid out, have no clearly defined purpose and do not even promote the author's own books particularly well.

The idea about the blog is that you have new content on a daily, or at least weekly basis, to help you connect with your readers and to build up your fan base. The idea is that you post up short stories, sample chapters, general articles about life, the universe and everything and hope that the world beats a path to your door: your web site acts as your shop window, your blog shows that you are a likeable person.

Personally, I do not have a blog. I rarely read anyone else's. I really question the claims made about their benefit and all too often I have seen blog pages that are unfocused, ramble and have no purpose. I suspect that very few blogs have actually repaid their investment in increased book sales for their owners.

Instead of having your own blog at your own blogsite, create a Facebook fan page and contribute to other blogs and forums. You instantly have an audience, and if you don't contribute to them for a few weeks, there is no harm done.

Furthermore, instead of posting short stories and articles onto a blog page, where they will be read once and then instantly discarded, why not package a few of them together and offer it either for sale as a free eBook? Nobody attaches value to a blog post. They do to a free eBook. You're therefore creating a much more powerful marketing tool to help you sell more books.

Social Networking

Facebook has twice as much internet traffic as Google and is used by over 250 million people around the world. People are three times more likely to look at your books based on personal recommendation from friends than from any other form of promotion. So make it easy for people to recommend your book on websites such as Facebook and Twitter.

Tell all your friends about your book on Facebook. Post up a message on Twitter and ask your followers to retweet it to their followers.

As a separate post on Facebook and Twitter, put a link to your video. If you do not catch people with the first message, you may well do with your second.

It is easy to be carried away with Twitter, searching for your key words, responding to people, and telling them about your book. If you decide you want to do this, please do not forget that Facebook and Twitter are not there for blatantly promoting your book. They are there for friends to talk to each other.

If you are blatantly advertising on Facebook and Twitter, you are likely to get a backlash from the rest of the social networking community. Use your discretion: if there is an appropriate Internet conversation going on and you have a social relationship with some of the people involved, then a discrete mention of your book may be appropriate.

There is a fine line between adding an appropriate comment and blatant advertising. Use your discretion, and if you do upset someone, apologize immediately.

You can very quickly lose a lot of time in Facebook and Twitter, and personally, I am not entirely convinced that the benefits make it worthwhile spending too much time on either. 'Little and often' appears to be the best approach. If you do join up and use Facebook and Twitter, do it primarily for social reasons and have fun. Do not kid yourself that you are 'doing marketing' when actually you are just chatting to friends.

Facebook Groups

You can create a 'fan page' in Facebook, either as an author's page or as a book page. This allows you to post up interesting information, quotes and snippets that may be of interest to your followers. Many writers use Facebook to post up short stories, flash fiction and comments about what they are working on. If you are trying to establish yourself in a particular genre then this can be a useful way of attracting followers over time.

You can also join other groups within Facebook. However, remember that Facebook is a social group and people visit Facebook to have fun, not to read your adverts. If you are a member of a group, be an active participant and do it for the enjoyment of being part of that group. Then you can mention to the group that you have an eBook that you would love people to read, but do not over promote it and annoy other people. They will very quickly switch off to you and your message.

However, do not spend too much time on Facebook and kid yourself that you are marketing. If you are writing a short story or a piece of flash fiction, do it because you want to write it rather than specifically for Facebook. Once you have written it, by all means post it up on your Facebook page if you want to and let other people enjoy it, but do not expect to sell hundreds of books just because you've written a short story and posted it on Facebook.

Getting your book promoted on other websites

You should already have a good idea of the sort of person who will be attracted to your book. People who own eBooks tend to be reasonably computer literate and are comfortable with using the world wide web. Many of them read blogs and informational websites, so your next step should be to get information about your book onto those sites.

Use Google and some suitable search terms for your book and look for blogs and informational sites that appear on the first three pages of your search. If you do not find anything suitable, try other search terms.

Getting your eBook onto blogs is often easy. Most bloggers are always on the lookout for interesting new content to get their readers coming back regularly. Your news is even better for the blogger: it gives them the chance to earn some money at the same time.

Send them an e-mail introducing yourself and your book and telling them exactly why your book will be of interest to their readers. Include a write-up that they can copy and paste into their blog, incorporating all your key words. Include a small photograph of yourself and an image of your book cover. Include a link to the video on YouTube and a link to the eBook on Amazon. Remind them that if they have their own Amazon Affiliate account, they can make money on every copy sold.

If you have a website that you can easily update, offer to put a link to their article on their website if they blog about your book. Tell them that you do not want a link back into your website (although if they do offer, do not turn them down!)

If you do not have the facility to do this, tell them that you will post a message on Facebook and Twitter thanking them and putting a link through to their article on their blog if they post up information about your eBook.

For every ten e-mails you send, you are likely to get two or three positive responses. Keep working at it. Very quickly you will end up getting a large number of sites promoting your book.

Informational sites are also quite keen to include press releases and announcements on their websites, especially if they can go on to make money through an Amazon Associate scheme on any copy of your eBook they sell.

Continue 'working the blogs' for several months. Sometimes you will find very few responses, other times you will get a lot. However, every time you get your eBook mentioned on a blog, along with some of your key words, you are increasing the amount of times your book gets exposure. It all helps to ensure that when someone searches for one of your key words in Google, it is your name and your eBook that gets to the top of the list.

Hyperlinks

As well as bloggers, you will find other websites that cater to a similar audience to your book, where they may not be particularly interested in promoting your book, but would be prepared to swap web links with your website.

Swapping web links between websites can work well to get your ranking up on Google and other search engines. If you find a website that has a similar target audience to your book, but where the site owner does not want to have an article about your eBook on their site, ask if you can swap links between websites. Provide a one-line description and a hyperlink that incorporates your most important key word combination and ask the other website to use this information when linking to your website.

This benefits both your website and their website. By providing a link to another interesting site, you are giving something more to your website visitors. They benefit in the same way. You also both benefit because Google will rank both sites higher in search listings, which means you will get more web visitors in general. Success breeds success.

E-mails

Everyone hates 'spam' e-mail, and for that reason, I would recommend you do not indulge in it. However, there are a few nice ways to promote your new book via e-mail. Remember, we are trying to promote your eBook in an open, honest and friendly way. Despite the reputation of spam, e-mails can be an excellent way of doing just this.

We all send e-mails all of the time. It is a great way of getting in touch with friends, family, colleagues and business associates. So why not send them an e-mail to tell them about how excited you are about your book, tell them where they can read a sample of the book for free (you can do this directly from your book page on the Amazon website) and ask them to spread the word amongst their friends and colleagues? Written in an open and friendly way, to people you already know, it can be a great way to get people talking about your book and gain some early sales.

E-mail signatures

All e-mail systems allow you to add a signature to the bottom of your e-mails. You send e-mails to friends, colleagues, associates and business partners.

Create an attention grabbing, single line description of your new book as part of your e-mail signature. Put in a link to allow people to find out more about your book.

This can act as a subtle reminder to your friends and associates that you have a book on sale. If they have not already bought a copy or told their friends about the book, an e-mail signature can remind them to do something about it.

Website communities and forums

Are you a member of any website communities or online forums? If so, you can often include a signature at the bottom of your posts in the same way as you can create e-mail signatures.

If you are an active and regular participant of these forums, and have been for some time (at least a couple of months), this can work extremely well to promote your book. Likewise, if you are already an active participant, you can probably post up a thread specifically about your eBook. If it is done in a friendly and open way, by someone that other people within that community already know and trust, then this is normally acceptable. If you are well liked within that website community, you will probably get some very positive responses from other forum members and some of them may buy your book.

Do not confuse this with signing up to website communities simply to promote your book, however. If you do this, you will end up with a bad reputation, which will not help you or your book. You will probably be kicked out of the forums. People do not visit these forums in order to be hit with lots of faceless advertising.

There are web forums everywhere and for every subject. If you join new forums, get yourself established first before promoting your book in any way. Answer people's queries, join debates and add thoughtful comments that extend the discussions. Make new online friends. Visit the forums regularly and get yourself known. Once you are getting yourself known within that particular community, then let them know about your book, but do not stop being a regular contributor to the forums in other ways.

Google Alerts

Google has another tool that is wonderful for authors, called Google Alerts. This allows you to be notified by e-mail whenever Google finds new internet content that contains specific key words.

You can find Google Alerts at

www.Google.com/alerts

Go to the site, enter a set of key words and your e-mail address and then once a day, Google will e-mail you a summary of all that is new on the internet that fits in with those key words.

Google Alerts is a very powerful facility. You can use it in two ways:

1. To find out where your book is being talked about on the web.

2. To see when your key words are being used on the web, so that you can contribute to a story.

Tracking what is happening to your book on the web

Quite often, I have found that somebody has mentioned my book on a forum, or in a blog. Because Google Alerts tells me when something has been posted, I can find out what has been said. If it is a forum or a blog posting where I can add a comment to the end of the post, I then have the option of contributing to the discussions if I think it is appropriate.

Tracking key words

If you are using Google Alerts to track your key word phrases, you can see all the other new content that is being picked up on those same key words. You can often find new sites that need to know about your book in this way, or if it is a blog or a forum, you can post up your own comments and add to the discussion, whilst adding a link to your book at the same time.

This strengthens your own website when Google scans that website again: you've added new, relevant content to that website and your link to your website strengthens your use of your key words.

Podcasts

A podcast is a fun and interesting way to get coverage. If you have never come across podcasting before, a podcast is a radio show that listeners download over the Internet. They can be listened to on a computer or an MP3 player.

Podcasts are usually released weekly or monthly. Some of them go on forever; others have a short run or else are produced in series. Some of them are presented by well-known celebrities, whilst others are presented by enthusiasts.

There are podcasts on every subject. Have you written a quiz book? There are several quiz podcasts available. Have you written a murder mystery? Then there are podcasts for you. In fact, whatever you have written your book about, there are almost certainly several podcasts that are dedicated to your genre.

You can find Podcasts at the iTunes website (www.iTunes.com) or by looking at any one of the number of Podcast Directories that you can find on the Internet.

There are both great podcasts and not-so-great podcasts, but inevitably, people who produce podcasts on a regular basis are always on the outlook for interviewees and for content. Why not offer to be a guest on a podcast?

Podcasts are also great practice for doing radio or television interviews. Once you have done a few podcasts, you will find that you present yourself better and are far more confident behind the microphone.

Do your research first. Go and listen to a few podcasts and find some that interest you and that you enjoy. Try to find out how popular they are: there is no point going on a podcast that has no audience!

You will typically carry out a podcast from the comfort of your own home and your own PC, using software such as Skype to talk to the interviewer. Get yourself a good microphone or headset and you are in business.

If you do go onto a podcast, remember you are not just there to plug your book. You will be expected to contribute. Do not see it as a formal interview. Rather, regard it as a chat between friends. Relax and smile and your voice will have natural warmth to it that always resonates well with listeners. Make sure you have a glass of water next to you so you do not get too dry and when you are not talking, press the mute button on your microphone (or on Skype) so that background noises are kept to a minimum.

If you are interesting, well informed and can debate well with other people, you will be a valuable addition to the show. It will help boost your reputation and help you build a new audience.

At the end of a podcast, the presenter will usually ask you about your eBook, and ask how people can get in touch with you. Give the name of your eBook, tell people it can be bought on Amazon and then tell people how they can find you: either with your website or via a Twitter or Facebook account.

Getting mainstream media coverage

There is a lot of work you can do with promoting your book outside the Internet. Much of this work will create sales 'spikes' where you sell most of your books over a period of a few days and then have very little ongoing benefit, but this is not always the case. If your book is reviewed by a newspaper or magazine, a summary of the article is likely to appear on their website. This can mean you get an initial spike, followed by a lower level of ongoing sales for several months.

Getting mainstream media coverage is never easy and should be regarded as a nice bonus rather than your principle form of book promotion. It is great when it happens and gives a good boost to the ego, but do not rely on it.

It is worth spending a little time working with the traditional media and making sure that you make it easy for journalists to get in touch with you.

Media Packs

When you have released your book, it is time to create a media pack. A media pack consists of the following:

- A press release about the book
- Authors bio
- A sample chapter from the book
- A photograph of the eBook cover
- A head and shoulders photograph of you

- Contact Information so that a journalist can get in touch with you quickly

Writing a press release

Writing a good press release is a skill of its own. It is a proven way of getting your story out to the traditional media. Whilst writing a press release does not guarantee that you will get your story published, not having a press release makes it a virtual certainty that you will not.

When writing a press release, you need to look at what you want to say objectively. Who is the audience? Does the press release contain invaluable or newsworthy information? What will readers learn from the press release?

Press releases need to be written in a newsworthy way. The content should be relatively short, punchy, interesting and concise. It needs to remain objective. Where possible and relevant, it should link in with a recent news story or topic.

Some authors struggle to write interesting, relevant and punchy press releases. If that is you, there is no shame in asking another writer to write a press release for you. Many freelance journalists write press releases for a reasonable price.

If you are writing your own press release, there is a tried and tested format for press releases:

The headline

Short, punchy and concise, the headline captures the reader's attention.

The subheading

Provides a context for your announcement.

Date and Location

Your press release must be dated. If your press release is regional, you can also include a location, typically a city and country.

If you are sending your press release to local newspapers and television and radio stations, it is a good move to include your location. If you are sending your press release elsewhere, a location is not always particularly relevant.

Information

This is the press release itself. They are typically between three and eight paragraphs in length. The first paragraph says what the press release is about and why it is important. The second paragraph provides more details or provides a quote from you. Subsequent paragraphs provide more details, but remember to keep it short, punchy and interesting.

The last paragraph should provide a brief bio and provide details of where readers can buy the book. Include hyperlinks to your website.

At the end of the press release, include a separate line with ###, which indicates that this is the end of the release. This allows an editor or journalist to scan the press release quickly and easily.

Contact Information

Provide a way for journalists to get in touch with you. This can be a telephone number and/or an e-mail address.

An example Press Release

Here is a press release that I issued recently for a series of books I wrote on electric cars:

<u>For immediate release</u>

Electrifying books drives information on Electric Cars

February 24, 2011 – A new series of electric car books has made their debut today. Their goal is to offer informative guides to people who are interested in owning an electric car.

The Electric Car Guides are a series of the most detailed and comprehensive range of books on electric car ownership available. The series covers everything from a general overview to specific guides on individual models. Best-selling author Michael Boxwell is a long-term electric car owner and provides readers with first-hand accounts, impressions and facts on these exciting, cutting-edge vehicles.

"I have been using electric cars on a daily basis for the past five years", says Boxwell. "The latest electric cars from companies like Nissan and Mitsubishi are fast, fun and provide a great driving experience. With ever-rising fuel costs, they also break our dependency on oil."

"The books also look at the environmental benefits of electric cars, contains a directory of all the electric cars you can buy today and contains testimonies from other electric car owners", he adds.

Although cars powered by electricity are nothing new, they are still in their infancy. The big manufacturers are now launching models and it is certain that the future looks bright for battery powered vehicles. But who are they aimed at? Why should consumers consider one? What are the advantages of battery power over the internal combustion engine? The Electric Car Guides provide prospective buyers the answers to these questions.

Boxwell has been involved with electric vehicles since 2003, originally running a company that promoted and sold battery-powered vehicles throughout the UK and Ireland. More recently, as the founder of one of the largest electric car clubs in the world, he talks with other people who use these cars every day. In addition, Boxwell regularly meets with the car manufacturers who are building these cars.

"Electric cars are an exciting alternative to traditional fossil fuel powered internal combustion engine cars. As electric cars debut on the market, promoted by the marketing campaigns of large auto manufacturers, consumers can benefit from an independent view of what these cars are genuinely like to use. As these vehicles make their transition from the labs and test tracks to the mainstream, understanding them before investing is an important step. We are excited to be among the first to offer that information", Boxwell emphasizes.

The series of Electric Car Guides are available from Amazon and all good booksellers, priced $14.99 in the United States and £9.99 in the United Kingdom. More information can be found at www.TheElectricCarGuide.com.

\#\#\#

Contact Information
For more information, contact Michael Boxwell directly on XXXXXXXXXX or by e-mail at XXXXXXXXXXXXXXX.

Author and book photographs available from www.GreenstreamPublishing.com/media.html

What to do with your media pack

Your media pack needs to be posted on your website, and the press release should be posted onto a free public relations 'wire' service.

A PR wire service is unlikely to be picked up by many mainstream newspapers or magazines straight away, but will be picked up by Google and the other search engines. Often the story will be picked up by a few bloggers and informational websites. If you are lucky, you may get a mention in a magazine or newspaper.

In the US, www.PRlog.com is a good free PR wire service; www.PRnewsWire.com is probably the best, but use the free service rather than the paid-for service, as it can otherwise get very expensive, very quickly.

For the UK, www.PRfire.co.uk provides an excellent wire service. This also has the benefit of being picked up by Google News, which can lead to a large number of web visitors very quickly.

For best results with a press release, you should also have a look for suitable newspapers, magazines and radio and TV shows to get in touch with to tell about your book. You can find newspapers and magazines in a newsagents or library. Make a note of the editor's name, e-mail address, phone number, and give them a call. Tell them in ten seconds that you have written an eBook and tell them the subject. Ask for permission to send a press release to them. The answer will be yes. Confirm their e-mail address and thank them. Sometimes you end up with a long conversation with the editor as well, and that can be great as it means they can see a story. If this happens, you are usually going to get some editorial of some sort.

Never ask an editor if they will definitely print something. It is unprofessional and puts them on the spot. As soon as you put the phone down, drop them an e-mail thanking them for their time. Send it immediately.

In around one in five cases, you will get a call or an e-mail back, asking for a review copy of your book. If you get this, it usually means you are going to get a review. Good reviews in a well read magazine or newspaper always results in increased sales. Many reviews also end up on the magazine or newspaper website as well, which means the long-term effect on sales can be very beneficial indeed.

Love Journalists

Journalists often have a very difficult job. Quite often, they have to research a subject extremely quickly and then write an article on a particular subject, with very little prior experience and with a very tight deadline.

If you have expertise that is covered in your book, you need to let journalists know about that expertise. If your book is a factual book, then often the expertise is obvious. With a fiction book, you will have some areas of expertise that may be of interest to a journalist on a particular story. Your expertise could be in storytelling, communicating with a particular section of society, or how to get people excited by poetry. Whatever it is, a journalist could be looking for someone with your knowledge right now.

Journalists and authors have a lot in common. There is a strong affinity between the two groups. If you talk to a journalist about a subject and they use the material, they will always identify you as the author of whatever book you are promoting, so you get some very worthwhile publicity at the same time.

To let journalists know about your areas of expertise, register with www.HelpaReporter.com and www.NewsBasis.com. These are free services that will regularly e-mail you summaries of what reporters are working on and the experts they want to interview. Both these services are mainly US based and can be a great way to get your message across in the United States. Subscribe to the service and monitor the e-mails regularly.

The power of FREE

Everyone likes getting something for free. The word FREE is a powerful one. It is not only associated with getting something for nothing, it is associated with freedom and of extraordinary value.

In short, you need to consider creating something of value that you can give away for free.

What you give away must have a value in the eyes of the recipient. Give someone something that they value, they will be grateful and will look for a way to repay you. Give something something of no value at all, both you and the gift will be dismissed.

Your free gift must be relevant. If you are selling a book on survival techniques in the Sahara, don't give away a knitting pattern! Make your free gift relevant, useful and interesting.

Packaging FREE

Many authors already give away something for free: their blog posts of short stories and ideas. You may get people reading your blogs, but they are unlikely to be valued: nobody ever pays to read a blog, so what is the true value of that blog?

Because people expect blogs to be free, you are unlikely to get people responding by wanting to give you something in return. Worse, your blog may be regarded as irrelevant, which means that you risk being ignored.

But what about giving away a free eBook? An eBook has a value. People pay for eBooks. So if you give away an eBook, you're giving away something of value. Presumably, as you have written it, it is also relevant and interesting as well.

Make sure that your free product also entices people to read your paid-for book. In the example of a free eBook, make sure you give the reader a buzz at the end of the book, make them genuinely excited to read more of your work and then tell them where they can get your next book. Remember, if they're reading an eBook, they will have just finished reading one book and will be eager to read the next one. Make sure it is easy for them to impulse buy yours.

When readers get in touch with you

If you have made it easy for your readers to get in touch with you, you are quite likely to get a steady trickle of responses over time.

You may be fearful that all you will get is a barrage of abuse or lots of e-mail spam, but my experience is exactly the opposite. You are far more likely to get people getting in touch to thank you for writing the book, to ask questions or to offer some constructive feedback.

It is always great to receive an e-mail from someone who has enjoyed the book. Fan mail is good for the soul, so long as you do not let it go to your head! If you do get a nice e-mail or message, write back straight away, thanking the sender for his thoughtful comments, tell them how it has brightened up your day and ask them if they would be happy to post up a review on Amazon to let other people know that they liked your book.

Do not be disheartened if you do get the occasional complaint. If you respond quickly and answer that person's complaint, you will normally get a much more positive response afterwards.

If you do receive the same criticism more than once, or receive a number of questions about the same topic, it may suggest that you need to create a revised edition of the book. Consider criticisms objectively and you can often benefit from them in the long term, but remember you cannot please everyone.

The nice thing about making yourself approachable to your readers is that you will usually get a lot more positive responses than negative. Unlike many other products, where people only write a review to complain about something, authors seem to get many responses that are more positive. Readers tend to respect authors. If your book is enjoyed by your readers, they will let you know.

Keep on keeping on

Too many authors launch their new book, 'do' marketing for a couple of weeks and then give up because they do not see any rewards.

Unfortunately, this is a recipe for failure. Promoting your book is best done little and often for several months. Do not try to run a marathon and burn yourself out after a few weeks.

There is no guarantee of success with your book. However, if you have written a good book and you promote it properly, you will almost always achieve sales.

Chapter 10: What happens next?

Do not expect miracles overnight, but if you continue to promote your eBook, you will start building your sales.

Every week you need to dedicate some time to promoting your book. Even half an hour a week is better than nothing is. Keep your eye out for new websites and new blogs that may be interested in your eBook. Create new videos for YouTube. Consider an audio book to promote on iTunes and Audible.com.

It can take six months for sales of your eBook to take off, so do not be disheartened if you only see slow sales after only a couple of months. Perseverance does pay when promoting your eBook.

The more references to your book that you get on different websites, the higher the ranking your book gets on Google. In turn, more people will get to find out about your book and the better your ranking gets on sites like Amazon.

Likewise, on Amazon, as more people look at your eBook, Amazon will promote your eBook to their customer base. They will do this by suggesting your eBook to customers browsing similar items and by directly emailing prospective readers promoting your book.

With Amazon, success does breed success and the more you promote and sell your book, the more Amazon will do to help you.

If you have your e-mail address or a contact form on your website, you will often get people who buy your eBook get in touch with you directly. If they say nice things about your book, ask them if they would mind writing a review for you on Amazon. Most happy customers who have taken the time to get in touch with you directly are delighted to write a review if you ask them.

Occasionally you may get a poor rating on Amazon. If your book is essentially good, that is nothing to worry about too much. If you get a poor review, you have the opportunity to respond to it on Amazon. If you do so, do not argue with the reviewer. Thank them for their frank review and answer their points politely and positively. Other people will see that you have responded and so even the occasional poor review can be made into a positive thing.

Of course, if you have written a poor book, you will end up with lots of poor reviews. At that point, there is no point continuing to promote your eBook. However, so long as you have written a good book, you have nothing to worry about from the occasional poor review. You can never please everybody all of the time. So long as the majority of your readers are happy with your book, you will always end up with many more good reviews than bad.

If you have a reviewer with a genuine gripe about the book, there is nothing stopping you going back to the book, improving it and uploading an update to Amazon. If you do this, make sure you post a response to the original review, thank them for reviewing the book and tell them that the book has been updated because of their valuable feedback.

Time to consider the printed book?

If your eBook has become successful and you do not have a printed edition of the book on sale, perhaps now would be a good time to produce one.

If you are already attracting some good sales for your eBook, getting a printed edition and increasing your sales is surprisingly easy. You will need to lay out your document to work in printed form and then work with a *Print on Demand* provider to get your book printed and on sale.

CreateSpace.com is one of the best known of the Print on Demand providers. For a set-up fee of around $40, you can upload your formatted book document to them. They will issue an ISBN number and put it on sale. CreateSpace books are sold on Amazon. The company handles all orders and deliveries themselves. At the end of each month, CreateSpace provide you with a statement of earnings and send you a royalty payment.

You can still earn a reasonable income from printed book sales. Publishing a printed book often gives you more credibility than an eBook. Having both editions linked together on Amazon enhances sales of both books, giving you twice the opportunity to sell your work to potential customers.

What if my book just is not selling?

If your book is just not selling after several months, you may be doing something wrong. It is most likely one of three things:

- Your presentation is wrong
- Your book is priced wrongly
- You are promoting the book to the wrong set of people

Of course, there is a fourth reason: your book is no good. If you are consistently getting poor reviews, it is time to withdraw the book from sale and start again.

If you are getting good reviews, but just not a lot of sales, it often boils down to one of those other reasons. So let us look at those other three reasons in more detail, and see what can be done about it:

Presentation

Look at your eBook cover. Does it stand out from other eBooks? Does it leap out on the screen at you, or does it look plain or confusing? If you are not happy with your book cover, maybe now it is time to redesign it.

Is there a clear message in the title and sub-title? Does it tell the buyer exactly why they should buy your book? If not, change your sub-title. Alternatively, consider re-releasing the book with revised content and a brand new title.

Look at your page on Amazon. Does it provide many reasons for the potential customer to choose your book? Is it well written, clear and concise?

How does your Amazon listing compare to listings of similar books from other authors? Make sure that your listing page is at least as good, as and preferably better than your direct competitors are.

Check your tags on your Amazon page. Are there any new key words you could use to associate with your book? If so, add them.

Look at your website. Does it look professional? Does it look interesting? Have you made it easy for people to buy your book?

Pricing

How does your book compare on price with similar books from other authors? If your book is more expensive, it is time to cut your prices. You may even consider dropping your price to under £1 / $1 for a limited time. This should boost your sales volumes, give you the opportunity to get more top reviews and get your book noticed.

If you do change your prices, do not change them too regularly, even if you are planning to do a special price for a limited time. If you reduce your price to under £1/$1, plan to do this for at least three months.

Promoting the book to the wrong set of people

Your book will not sell if you have been promoting the book to the wrong set of people.

Ask some trusted friends or other authors to suggest markets for your book. Come up with a new set of key words, modify your web pages, contact everyone who has previously blogged about your book, and give them something newsworthy for them to publish it again.

If all else fails...

Of course, some books sell better than others do. It is not always clear why. If your book stubbornly refuses to sell despite positive reviews and great publicity, start again with your next book.

When your new book is published, update the content of your current book to include a promotion for your new book in it. Then update your current book to include a promotion for your new one at the end of the book and make it a free giveaway. You will not make any money on it, but if it has received good reviews, people will download it and read it. If they like it, they may then buy your new eBook, so you will end up earning money out of your original eBook by using it to promote your new one.

In conclusion

Once you have released your eBook, you will need to keep an eye on how it is doing for the lifetime of that eBook. Respond to customers when they get in touch, monitor reviews and do some promotions just to keep the momentum going.

If your eBook is successful, you may wish to consider releasing an audiobook version or a printed book if you do not have one already.

If your book is not selling, there are steps you can take to rectify the problem. If all else fails, do not be disheartened. Write another book and use your first book as a way of promoting the second.

Chapter 11: Creating an EPUB format eBook

In my opinion, this is an optional step. It may well become more important in the coming year as more e-readers are sold and if the Apple iBookStore becomes more popular amongst Apple iPad, iPhone and iPod owners.

Right now, your eBook is on sale on the largest bookshop in the world, working with the most popular eBook-reading format, Kindle. You are working with a retailer who will promote your book and give you the same opportunities to sell your book as they give to the big book publishers.

Once you have started building up momentum with your new eBook, you may decide to provide your book in the EPUB format and have it distributed on other bookseller's websites.

Getting your book on Kindle does not restrict you to simply offering a Kindle eBook version. You can offer other eBook versions through other retailers, such as Barnes & Noble (who sell the NOOK e-reader), Waterstones, Borders and the Apple iBookStore.

In the same way that Amazon makes it easy to offer a Kindle version of your eBook, there are a number of companies that you can work with in order to get your eBook formatted and into the distribution channel.

A word about Digital Rights Management on EPUB books

With the Kindle, Digital Rights Management (DRM) is not a huge issue for customers. Very few Kindle owners would choose not to buy a book just because it has DRM enabled.

To recap, Digital Rights Management means that a customer cannot freely distribute your eBook to other people: it is locked down to work only on devices registered to that customer.

With EPUB format books, however, DRM is a real issue. Many people absolutely refuse to buy eBooks with Digital Rights Management enabled and your sales may suffer if you have Digital Rights Management enabled.

When you ask people why this is the case with EPUB books, you will get all sorts of excuses. Some people say that the whole DRM concept treats customers like criminals by demanding they register their copy of the book to themselves. Other people will say it infringes on their rights, or that it stops them from lending eBooks to their friends in the same way that they might lend a paperback.

Yet none of this is a problem with Kindle books, so why is there an issue with EPUB books?

The real reason for this is that DRM on EPUB makes it difficult to use the eBooks. The two main software packages that are available to read DRM-enabled eBooks are Adobe Digital Editions and the Sony e-reader software.

Early editions of Adobe Digital Editions were clunky and awkward to use. The software crashed regularly. Later versions are better, but are still not particularly reliable or easy to use. It also has a habit of inexplicably losing its configuration so that it will no longer work with an e-reader. Some people also complain that it slows down the performance of their PC.

The Sony e-reader software is far worse. Many users have trouble even getting the software to install on their PC. It is very unstable, crashes regularly and many people find it entirely unusable.

Without one of these two pieces of software, it is impossible to register yourself as the legitimate user of a DRM-enabled eBook. So many people simply avoid using them at all. This means they simply cannot read DRM-enabled eBooks.

If the software suppliers had done a competent job of writing their e-reader software, in the way that Amazon has done with the Kindle, there would have been no big fuss made about DRM on eBooks. Everyone would have accepted DRM as a fair way to deliver eBooks to customers.

Unfortunately, the reality is that DRM with EPUB books is a total mess. If you use DRM with EPUB format books, many people cannot read them on their e-readers. You therefore restrict your market quite considerably if you use DRM with EPUB books.

If you are not prepared to waive Digital Rights Management, you are wasting your time producing an EPUB book.

Reading EPUB books on your PC or Mac

As part of the checking process, you are going to have to be able to read EPUB format books on your PC or Mac. The industry standard software for doing this is Adobe Digital Editions, which is available free of charge from the Adobe website (http://www.adobe.com/products/digitaleditions/). This will allow you to see what your eBook looks like when formatted into EPUB format.

More formatting required

When you start working with a company on different versions of your eBook, you will need to modify some of your formatting in order to work with their own standards.

If nothing else, you will need to change the words 'KINDLE EDITION' from your title page to something more appropriate. For instance, if you use Smashwords, they ask you to use the words 'SMASHWORDS EDITION' on your title page.

Some of this formatting requires some experimentation. If you have done a good job of formatting your Kindle book, then you may have little or no formatting problems when converting your book to EPUB format. However, each of the formatting tools from each company has its own idiosyncrasies. Carefully check the converted documents to make sure that your eBook looks great when converted to EPUB format.

Some companies require you to pay for converting your book to the EPUB format and simply handle the distribution process, others offer a full end-to-end solution and do not charge extra for the conversion process.

Using third-party tools to convert your book to EPUB format

There are online tools available to help you convert your Word document to EPUB format. I particularly like www.2epub.com, who allows me to convert my books free of charge. The 2epub tool produces an excellent result and is more reliable than many of the paid-for services I have used in the past.

Just as with the Kindle conversion, there may well be some issues with the layout of your book using these third-party tools, so you need to check them carefully once conversion is completed by downloading them to your PC and reading through them.

Smashwords

www.Smashwords.com

Smashwords is one of the biggest EPUB publishing sites, allowing you to earn up to 60% commission on each sale and distribution through Apple's iBookStore, Sony and a number of American booksellers such as Barnes and Noble and Borders.

The Smashwords system does not just limit your book to EPUB format. You can also publish your book in a number of other formats as well, including PDF, HTML and even straight text. This flexibility means that if you work with Smashwords, you will end up with an eBook that will work for everyone, no matter what system they are using to read it.

The Smashwords system is very easy to use and allows you to get an eBook on to the market within a few minutes. The site offers step-by-step instructions and a clearly written instruction manual can be downloaded from the site.

Smashwords do not allow you to have the option of DRM. If you publish a book with Smashwords, you have to keep your book open.

You do not need to use a third-party conversion tool such as 2epub to work with Smashwords. You submit Word documents to Smashwords directly. They convert and format your book online using their own software.

The Smashwords tool does have some limitations. It does not support tables, columns or tabs. If your document includes any of these, you need to consider how else to present the information so that this is no longer an issue. You can import tables as images, or consider presenting the information in graphical form with a chart or diagram.

Smashwords has some excellent online documentation. If you decide you want to work with Smashwords, spend an hour or two reading all their documentation first. You will find the whole process a whole lot easier.

I personally like Smashwords. They are an open, friendly, honest and approachable company. They have created a happy community of authors and customers.

Lulu

www.Lulu.com

Lulu is a self-publishing company who produce and distribute both printed books and eBooks. They offer many of the same benefits as professional publishing and distribution companies such as Lightning Source (see below), with a much more author-friendly front end, allowing you to produce both printed books and eBooks extremely easily.

Like Smashwords, Lulu provides eBook distribution to all the major Internet based booksellers. Unlike Smashwords, you need to handle all the file conversions to EPUB and PDF formats yourself, or pay Lulu to do it for you.

Prices for converting your documents start from $99 and go up to $299 for their standard service. For complicated books, Lulu can charge for additional time at the rate of $100 per hour. Lulu says that it takes around four to six weeks to get your EPUB format book completed.

The benefit of paying for the conversion is that you get a book that is properly formatted and accepted for publication. The downside is the upfront cost and the amount of time it takes to get your eBook converted.

Of course, you do not have to pay for conversion. You can format your book using the 2epub system and upload the converted files direct onto Lulu.

Like Smashwords, Lulu offer excellent support by way of online articles that you can read in order to get up to speed quickly. They also offer another benefit: you can produce a printed book as well as an eBook, and get it distributed through Amazon and other online bookshops.

Lightning Source

www.LightningSource.com

Lightning Source is a professional publishing support company used by many of the biggest publishers in the world. Owned by Ingram, the biggest publishers in the world, they offer professional print on demand facilities and worldwide distribution for printed books, and excellent eBook distribution facilities.

However, they are a company who are set up for the publishing industry, not directly with authors. If you want to work with Lightning Source, *you* become the publisher. You need to format your books in EPUB format before you start, you have to apply for an account, sign distribution contracts and provide ISBN numbers for your eBooks.

In return, you gain access to one of the best distribution channels for eBooks in the world. You set your own discount levels and you have greater control in how your book is distributed.

However, it is not easy to produce eBooks with Lightning Source. Even some publishing companies that produce paperback books with Lightning Source decide to go elsewhere for publishing eBooks.

Like Lulu, you need to provide eBooks in EPUB format already. There is a setup fee of $40 per eBook, plus a cataloguing fee of $11 per title per year.

If you make a mistake when submitting your book, it will be rejected by Lightning Source. You will have to pay another $40 to submit the book again.

The company is set up to deal with experienced book and eBook publishers. Their support system is not set up to cope with small self-publishers who may struggle with the basics. Lightning Source is a professional company set up to cater for professional publishers. If you do not want to play that game – and frankly as an individual author, you probably do not – then it is best to look elsewhere.

This all may sound very discouraging for Lightning Source, but it is not all bad news. Lightning Source is an excellent company for professional publishers. There are world leaders in the publishing industry because they are the best at what they do.

My recommendation is this: if you are an individual author, look elsewhere. If you are a publisher looking to produce large numbers of eBook titles, you have just found your ideal partner.

The best route to market

For my money, either Lulu or Smashwords offers the easiest and most efficient way to get my eBooks to market. Both of them offer excellent distribution models to all of the top bookstores and both of them offer good online support and services.

I have a huge respect for Lightning Source, but I am not the right customer for them as far as eBook publishing is concerned. As I have previously said, they are set up to work with publishers and if you are a publishing company, you should beat a path to their door.

Marketing your EPUB books

Your EPUB books are going to sell in different outlets to your Kindle books. You need to ensure that your EPUB book is presented as well as possible in these other online bookshops.

The biggest online bookshops outside of Amazon are Barnes and Noble and Borders in the United States, Waterstones, W.H. Smiths, Blackwell's and The Book Depository in the United Kingdom, and the Apple iBookStore on iTunes.

The key to sales of your eBook is to make sure you have reviews on each of these sites. As with Amazon, do not be tempted to make up your own reviews. You will be found out. Reread the reviews section on chapter 9 and carry out the same process with these other sites.

If you asked some of your friends or other authors to write reviews on Amazon, ask them if they would be prepared to write reviews for other sites.

If I am asking someone to write a second review on a different site, I tend to offer a book token in return, not as a bribe but simply as an acknowledgement that I am putting them out. After all, I am going to benefit from having the review against my book, so it is only fair that I give something back in return.

If you have published your book through Smashwords, they have a number of additional tools that you can use to help promote your book.

For a start, Smashwords has a community of authors with their own forums. Get involved and ask other authors what they have done to market their books. Read some other books on the Smashwords website and write reviews about them. If you are prepared to give a little yourself, you are more likely to receive back reviews in return.

Smashwords has a voucher scheme that you can use to offer discounts for your book, or even to offer your book free of charge to people who have a voucher. Vouchers can be limited so they are only used once, or used for a fixed period of time.

This can be a great way to give away copies of your books to reviewers, or as prizes for competitions, or to offer time-limited discounts to potential customers.

In conclusion

There are various options for producing different versions of your eBook to sell elsewhere. Right now, you will not see significant eBook sales because of your additional efforts, but that could change in the very near future.

It is not practicable to use Digital Rights Management to secure EPUB formatted eBooks.

If you produce additional versions of your eBook, you will need to spend time promoting them and marketing them in addition to the promotional work you have already done with your Kindle eBook.

A final word

Writing books is addictive. If you have written one, it is only a matter of time before you write a second. Then a third, followed by a fourth.

Take this book, for example. I have written two books in the past six months and had not intended to write another book just yet.

The thought of writing this *particular* book had not even occurred to me. It all started with me offering to do a short presentation to my local Writers' Group on eBooks. I wrote up some notes. I expanded on them. I added a bit here, a bit more there... before I knew it, I had written an entire book!

Whether you are a published author, or are still looking for that first publishing contract, producing an eBook makes a lot of sense. Not only can you get your books to market quickly, but also you are tapping into the fastest growing book market there is today. Your eBooks will go into an international market. You can make a name for yourself around the world.

You also have the opportunity to earn a nice income from your eBooks. Unless you are ultra successful and just a bit lucky, you will probably not earn enough money from just one eBook title to be able to live off that income. If you have a few titles to your name, however... well, that may be a different story.

Remember: the skills you learn from promoting your eBooks can also be applied to your printed books. If you already have printed books published, your publisher will also love the fact that you promote your books professionally and effectively. They will consider those when it comes to negotiating your contract for your next book (and if they do not, remind them!).

If you are new to eBooks, I hope this has given you the enthusiasm and knowledge to create one for yourself. Of course, it can be hard work, but the results can be fantastically rewarding, and not just in a financial sense.

Once you have written and launched your eBook, write to me and let me know about it. The MakeAnEbook website contains an eBook directory, and I'll be delighted to include your book in it. You'll get a valuable link into your website and another opportunity to promote your book.

I cannot promise to read every eBook, but I will gladly check out your website or Amazon listing and make comments on how you can improve them if you want me to. I can be contacted at www.MakeAnEbook.org.

If you are after more marketing ideas, I also present a Web TV series all about marketing your book. It's called *Book Marketing in 30 Seconds* and you can subscribe to it, free of charge, via iTunes or watch it on YouTube. Each episode lasts just 30 seconds and contains a tip or a technique to help you promote and market your book more successfully. Many of them are already covered in this book, but marketing is always evolving and you'll hear the very latest information via this series.

Finally, I have tried hard to give you all the information you need to get going, but if you feel that I have missed anything out or not explained something clearly enough, please let me know.

All the best with your next book,

Michael Boxwell
June, 2011
www.MakeAnEbook.org

Index

Lightning Source UK Ltd.
Milton Keynes UK
UKOW01f0926121213

222889UK00007B/209/P